GETTING READY TO TEACH FIRST GRADE

Written by Jadie S. Workman

Photos by Bruce Hazelton

Illustrated by Jenny Campbell

Rosalie Cochran

Judy Ciampa

We warmly thank the community of the Fern Avenue School of Torrance, California, especially Mrs. Rosalie Cochran, principal; Mrs. Judy Ciampa, first-grade teacher; and students, parents, and caregivers of Mrs. Ciampa's first-grade class.

Project Manager: Barbara G. Hoffman
Editor: Bob Newman
Book Design: Anthony D. Paular
Cover Design: Anthony D. Paular
Pre-Press Production: Daniel Willits and Randy Shinsato

FS122003 Getting Ready to Teach First Grade
All rights reserved—Printed in the U.S.A.
23740 Hawthorne Blvd.
Torrance, CA 90505

Let us put our minds together and see what life we can make for our children.

–Tatanba Iotanko, Sitting Bull, Lakota Sioux, 1877

CHAPTER ONE: INTRODUCTIONS

It may sound strange, but I think I already know some things about you. You're probably getting ready to teach first grade—maybe for the first time. That's great! Remember, every first-grade teacher was once a *first-year*, first-grade teacher. Soon you will agree that teaching first graders is a unique, exciting, and fulfilling role. You're probably slightly anxious about the upcoming year, and so you purchased this book, hoping for some new ideas and encouragement. Not to worry—I wrote this book with you in mind.

As the title suggests, this book will help guide your preparations for teaching first grade. It is intentionally practical, addressing topics new teachers and teachers in new grade levels ask most frequently. In addition to helpful information regarding classroom management, organization, and professional relationships, you will find examples and reproducible pages for lesson plans, class projects, field trips, and other activities. So what are you waiting for? Let's get ready to teach first grade!

INTRODUCTION TO THE STUDENT

Students begin first grade with a high degree of anticipation. Having spent their previous year in kindergarten, which was most likely a half-day in duration, these five-, six-, or seven-year-old children are excited about being at school all day like the older students. Yet getting adjusted to a full day is not the only major transition these children are undertaking. They are also exploring and determining the kinds of roles they play in school and with their peers.

Kindergarten introduces beginning students to a variety of social arrangements outside the home, and first graders will continue to develop skills in interacting with their peers. They begin to form groups of friends and establish new "best friends" relationships. These groups are seldom boy-girl groups, and they tend to change frequently. While peers are very important to first-grade students, they still look to adults for affirmation, guidance, and support.

First graders thrive on a teacher's demonstration of approval, encouragement, and support. Often affectionate toward the teacher, these children tend to behave in accordance with their perception of the teacher's values and attitudes. Therefore, we strive to reinforce each student's sense of self-worth. The first-grade experience can heavily influence a child's attitude toward school for his or her remaining years of education.

First graders show much enthusiasm about learning and are eager to participate in most classroom activities—largely because each experience in school is new. They continue to learn the relationship between rules, behavior, and consequences or rewards. Typically, students become more independent, goal-directed, and self-confident in first grade.

Physically, girls often demonstrate slightly higher levels of development and achievement than boys. However, all students' small muscle skills and eye-hand coordination will improve during the first grade. They will learn to draw recognizable human shapes and develop the physical skills needed for playing games. Physical exercise is important because first graders possess amazingly high energy levels.

Academically, first graders show obvious growth in all subject areas. During the year, they develop their language and thinking skills. They learn to remember multiple ideas simultaneously, order objects according to size and quantity, increase their attention span, and think more clearly about thoughts and judgments. At the same time, they learn how words and pictures represent reality, they comprehend the difference between past and present, and they develop a deeper understanding of language. This is the year in which children are ready for beginning reading and writing.

Our effectiveness as educators is directly related to how well we understand our students. Let's always keep in mind the developmental stages that our students experience, both in the classroom and at home. First graders are very impressionable. We have a tremendous opportunity to instill a love for learning into each of our first-grade students!

> **We can best understand learning as growth, an expanding of ourselves into the world around us. We can also see that there is no difference between living and learning, that living is learning, that it is impossible, and misleading, and harmful to think of them as being separate.**
>
> **—John Holt, What Do I Do Monday?, 1970**

OVERVIEW OF CURRICULUM FOR FIRST GRADE

This section is presented in alphabetical order by content area. The sequence is Language Arts, Mathematics, Multicultural Education, Physical Education, Science and Health, Social Studies, Technology, and Visual and Performing Arts (which includes Music).

In this overview section you will read about the concepts that are to be addressed in first grade. In Chapter Two—Bringing the Curriculum to Life—you will find a list of skills by content area generally accepted as appropriate for first grade. Following the lists of skills, you will find activities that you can use to teach the skills.

The content and curriculum information presented in this book is provided as a reference. It is not intended to replace your school or district's course of study or curriculum guides. Ask your principal or other supervisor for a list of the standards, frameworks, or "essential learnings" with which you align your lesson plans. In many cases, these standards will be used in measuring both students' skill levels and progress, as well as your own teaching effectiveness. Therefore, it is important to use these standards throughout the school year to make certain that all required skills are addressed. As additional references, you should read the standards published by national teacher organizations such as the National Council of Teachers of Mathematics. Your school or district resource centers will probably have copies of the National Standards documents you can use as references.

Parts of the curriculum sections of this book are based on the Standards of the National Council of the Teachers of Mathematics, the National Council of the Teachers of English, and the National Research Council of the National Academy of Sciences. Other references used are state frameworks and school district curricula from Illinois, California, Nebraska, Massachusetts, Washington, and New York.

Language Arts

Language Arts is a broad area of the curriculum which includes reading, writing, listening, and speaking. Through each of these processes, students express what they know, what they think and what they value about the world. They make connections between information they know and information they don't know.

Your school or district may have adopted textbooks or other language arts programs that include grammar, spelling, phonics, activity, and workbooks, or there may be specific guidelines you are expected to follow. Check with the curriculum coordinator or principal at your school before the school year begins.

Concepts

- Language is used to communicate ideas across time and space.

- Language allows us to express our life experiences and to give names and labels to what we know and value.

- Language allows us to express our feelings in a variety of ways.

- Language allows us to share what we understand about ourselves and about others.

3

Three components are important to developing the art of language in your classroom. The first is the use of literature, the second is easy access to many books and other educational media, and the third is an emphasis on writing as a process.

Literature

Books create a bridge between the "real world" and your classroom, and between different curricular areas. Good literature can make any information interesting and accessible. It is used to reinforce skill and concept development across the curriculum, and to extend new ideas into new contexts. Literature can arouse curiosity. It is essential for vocabulary development and learning how to think.

Library Media Resources

Your students should have regular access to a variety of materials from which they can select according to their own interests. You will need to develop a classroom library as well as use the resources of the school and local public libraries.

Writing

The process of speech-to-print is crucial to language development. The writing process includes several stages—prewriting, drafting, receiving responses, revising, editing, and, in many cases, postwriting. Through the writing process students develop their writing and related skills. They also improve their spoken language through discussion of their work and the work of others.

Processes

Students tell, retell, illustrate, describe, and share personal responses to class experiences. Teach everyday, idiomatic language—the language that your students hear around them. Phonemic awareness is continued as students make the connection between the words they hear and the words they read.

> We must go beyond what we were taught and teach how we wish we had been taught. We must bring to life a vision of what a mathematics classroom should be . . . A richer mathematics program is also supported by an explosion of new mathematical knowledge—more mathematics has been created in this century than in all our previous history.
>
> —Miriam A. Leiva, <u>Curriculum and Evaluation Standards for School Mathematics, Addenda Series</u>

Mathematics

First-grade students acquire number sense through a wide range of activities. They begin to develop a conceptual framework for understanding the properties and relationships of addition and subtraction. Mathematical vocabulary and language skills develop and are internalized as students discuss their discoveries, and then record their experiences using pictorial or numerical representations. They begin to tell time, conduct simple probability experiments, and use standard and non-standard measurement. Problem-solving skills and strategies are applied throughout the curriculum. Students explore and work with number patterns.

Concepts

- Classifying and sorting is based on identifying a specific attribute or attributes.

- Real objects and abstract shapes have one, two, and/or three-dimensional features which can be examined, compared, and analyzed. Geometric shapes have specific attributes and properties by which they are identified, classified, and named. The geometric shapes can be described in terms of their relative size, position, congruence, and similarity with other shapes.

- Measurement enables us to attach a number to a quantity using a unit which is chosen according to the properties of the quantity to be measured. Selection of an appropriate measuring tool requires considering the size of what is to be measured and the use of the measure.

- Identification of a rule that is used to generate a pattern enables one to extend that pattern indefinitely. The same patterns can emerge from a variety of settings.

- Questions that cannot be answered by direct observation can be assessed often by gathering data that often generates additional questions. Data can be gathered about every member of a group, or a representative sample from that group can be used. Data can be organized, represented, and summarized in a variety of ways.

- Numbers can be used to describe quantities and relationships between quantities. Any number can be described in terms of how many of each group there are in a series of groups. The four basic operations relate to one another and are used to obtain numerical information.

Multicultural Appreciation

Students in first grade are developing a self-identity and an awareness of ethnic heritage. They are also acquiring interpersonal skills. Some of the concepts they learn about during multicultural studies are listed below. These concepts should be integrated throughout the curriculum on a daily basis.

Concepts

- People are different from one another through physical, personality, and behavioral characteristics.

- Names are an important part of one's identity.

- Culture is taught through a family's language, beliefs, and traditions.

- Values and beliefs can be taught through music, art, and literature.

- Dignity and worth are found in each human being.

- People communicate and cooperate to maintain healthy relations.

- Feelings and emotions are controllable.

- People can be hurt by mean words.

Curricular activities should build the student's intellectual and interpersonal skills. These activities should include defining oneself as a member of different kinds of groups, showing positive gender roles, and developing a cultural identity. The students should identify similarities and differences in different cultural groups, learn the achievements of people of diverse cultural groups that have made a difference to others, listen to others, and share their own feelings. Correct terminology should be used to identify various racial and ethnic groups. Above all respect should be shown for all cultures.

Physical Education

First graders are ready for more complex games than they played in kindergarten. They should be exposed to goal setting. Some of your students may be beginning to participate in recreational sport activities.

Concepts

- **Motor Skills** The body can move in a variety of ways. Movement can occur at different paces and for durations of time. Movements may be continued.

- **Physical Fitness** The body is healthier when it is physically active on a regular basis. A person performs better when the body is physically fit. A person feels better when the body is physically fit.

- **Self-Image** A person performs best when he or she feels like a worthwhile person. Goal-setting leads to improved performance. Many attempts or practice experiences may be necessary in order to attain goals.

- **Social Behavior** The democratic process of majority decision making is practiced in many game situations. Good sportsmanship consists of following the game rules and showing encouragement to others. The acceptance of positive suggestions from one's teacher and others improves performance.

- **Recreational Interest** People can use their leisure time in a productive manner which keeps them physically fit. People participate in leisure time activities throughout their lives.

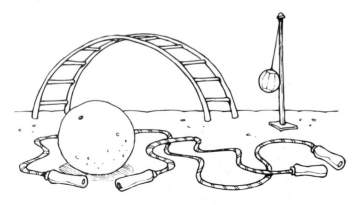

Science and Health

Science
Concepts
Most state education standards and frameworks are written based on the National Science Education Standards (NSES). The NSES presents its content standards by grade ranges, K-4, 5-8, and 9-12. Consequently, specific first-grade science study topics vary considerably from state to state and district to district. The NSES K-4 content standards published in 1996 follow. The science curriculum of your school or district will most likely be written to reflect these content standards.

Unifying Concepts and Processes
- Systems, order, and organization
- Evidence, models, and explanation
- Change, constancy, and measurement
- Evolution and equilibrium
- Form and function

Science as Inquiry
- Abilities necessary to do scientific inquiry
- Understandings about scientific inquiry

Physical Science
- Properties of objects and materials
- Position and motion of objects
- Light, heat, electricity, and magnetism

Life Science
- Characteristics of organisms
- Life cycles of organisms
- Organisms and environments

Earth and Space Science
- Properties of earth materials
- Objects in the sky
- Changes in the earth and sky

Science and Technology

- Abilities to distinguish between natural objects and objects made by humans

- Abilities of technological design

- Understanding about science and technology

Science in Personal and Social Perspective

- Personal health

- Characteristics and changes in populations

- Types of resources

- Changes in environments

- Science and technology in local challenges

History and Nature of Science

- Science as a human endeavor

Sample Curriculum

First graders improve their processes of observation, discrimination, and accurate description of objects and events through investigation of matter, living organisms, energy, and space. Students identify the properties of a broader range of non-living and living things. They become more familiar with the basic needs of plant and animal life, and the necessity for the humane treatment of animals. Through exploration of magnets, electricity, and heat, students become aware of the relationship of energy to their everyday worlds. An introduction to the solar system helps students understand concepts of day and night, temperature changes and weather. Students use science, reading, language arts, and mathematics, as well as other subject area processes and skills, to develop the science concepts.

Below you will find a sample curriculum that reflects concepts frequently presented in first grade.

Science

Life Science

- Plants and animals, including mammals, may be described and classified by similarities and differences in structural and behavioral characteristics.

- There is great diversity among animals; however, animals have similar basic needs.

- Human beings are mammals with needs and functions similar to those of other mammals.

- Living organisms have structures with specific adaptations and functions.

- Organisms reproduce their own kind.

- Life cycles vary among different animals.

- Living organisms change with time.

Physical Science

- Materials and objects have characteristics by which they can be described and classified.

- Matter exists as solid, liquids, and gas. It changes state with the addition or loss of heat.

- A force is a push or pull and is necessary to move an object or to stop an object already in motion.

- Gravity is the force that attracts objects to the center of the Earth.

- Electricity is an energy source used to run machines and provide light and heat.

- Magnets can attract objects.

- Magnets have two poles. Opposite poles attract; like poles repel.

- Heat, which is measured by temperature, comes from a variety of sources, including sun, fire, light, and friction.

Earth Science

- The sun is our closest star and is a source of heat and light.

- Earth rotates on its own axis in 24 hours, a motion that causes the succession of night and day.

> **Learning science is something that students do, not something that is done to them. "Hands-on" activities are not enough. Students must have "minds-on" experiences as well.**
>
> —National Science Education Standards, 1996

- Changes in the earth's surface over time are caused by nature and the activities of human beings.

- Rocks have characteristics by which they can be described and classified. Soils are formed from rocks.

- Earthquakes occur when parts of the earth move.

- Safety precautions taken in advance can reduce injury to people and damage to property when natural disasters occur.

- Air is all around us. Wind is moving air.

- Weather phenomena affect living things.

- Clouds have characteristics by which they can be described.

Health

Health concepts and skills can be studied as part of your language arts, math, science, and arts programs, as well as a separate unit of study.

Concepts

- Personal good health is more desirable than illness and demands a life-long investment. A balanced program of physical activities, rest, recreation, and adequate diet are essential to fitness and cardiovascular health. Protection and care for eyes, ears, mouth, teeth, gums, and posture promote general health and appearance.

- There are many different kinds of families. One family member's health affects the rest. Heredity and environment influence the development of living organisms. We can appreciate ourselves and others if we understand human growth and development through the life cycle.

- We must eat right to be healthy. Our environment (friends, family resources, life styles) reflects similarities and differences of food choices.

- The process of making a thoughtful decision reduces stress and anxiety, gives us self-respect and the respect of others, and provides us personal satisfaction. We must know, like, and understand ourselves; make friends; and get along with people to be mentally and emotionally healthy. If we understand and cope with emotions in an acceptable way, we can avoid the stress and anxiety of unresolved conflict.

- Drugs are substances that change the way the mind and body work. Medicines are drugs that can help the body. Other drugs can harm the body.

- Many factors contribute to diseases and disorders. How much we can control and prevent disease varies.

- Individuals are responsible for their own health and for knowing when to seek help from others. The community provides health-care resources. There are many careers in the field of health. A relationship exists between the quality of the environment and human health. We must all work to create and maintain a safe and healthful environment.

- Many accidents can be prevented. Each of us needs to be prepared to act effectively in times of emergency, including life-threatening situations. Safety measures can help reduce accidents and save lives.

Social Studies

The goal of a balanced elementary social studies program is to prepare students to participate in society with the knowledge, skills, and civic values that allow them to be actively and constructively involved. First-grade students learn about and explore the world in which they live. They learn that accepting responsibility allows for active participation in the family, the classroom, and beyond. They explore the interdependence of all people in a culturally diverse world and where they as individuals fit into it. Social studies is interdisciplinary. Many social studies concepts and skills can be studied as part of your language arts, math, science, and arts programs, as well as a separate unit of study.

Concepts

- The ways that families now and long ago meet/met their needs are in some ways similar and in some ways different.

- Fair play and good sportsmanship are elements of respect for the rights of others.

- A person's culture is defined by when, where, and how his or her ancestors lived. Cultural events and celebrations are important examples of cultural heritage.

- Geographic designations like city, state, and country help us think about places and their relative locations.

- Families depend upon one another and upon neighborhood services such as police, the fire department, the post office, markets, the harbor, and airport. How goods and services are used and acquired depends on supply and demand.

- Families, schools, and communities have rules, rights, and responsibilities. Our way of government balances rules, rights, and responsibilities and provides communities with the power to govern while protecting individual rights. A good citizen accepts individual responsibility for his or her own ethical behavior.

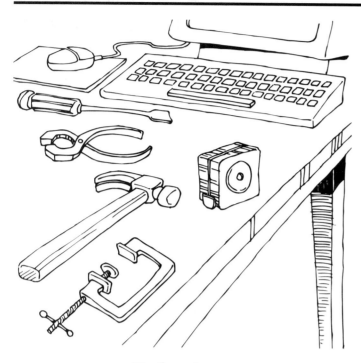

Technology

Technology can be broadly divided into two areas. One is industrial technology—learning construction processes and skills using wood, paper, cardboard, and plastic. The other is computer technology—learning fundamental computer concepts and tools. Curriculum development in this area is changing as fast as computer technology is. Many states and school districts are developing their academic standards in this field as this book goes to press. Check with your school or district.

Concepts

- Humans have changed their environments through technology.

- Materials and tools used repeatedly enable one to be more successful at a task.

- Directions and rules are part of our society.

- Numerous materials and tools are used to produce a product.

- Safety needs to be practiced every day.

- Many careers in technology are interrelated.

Visual Arts and Music

Visual Arts

First graders as a group present a tremendous variety in the patterns of their growth and development. They will be developing more fully the skills and concepts to which they were introduced in kindergarten.

Concepts

- The world can be perceived and described with images and symbols with visual and tactile qualities.

- Originality and personal experience are important to visual expression. Visual arts media can be used to communicate feelings and ideas.

- Art has played an important role in every culture throughout history. Studying art can give us insight into other people's lives.

- Using objective criteria for analysis, interpretation, and judgment based on aesthetic values results in informed responses to art and improved art production.

Music

Most students entering first grade will not be able to sing in tune. They will enjoy joining in imitative vocal activities which will strengthen and improve their voices. You will teach concepts and skills for in-tune singing, feeling for beat and accent, identifying rhythm patterns in familiar songs and to step and clap rhythm patterns in familiar songs, and to step and clap rhythmically. Children should understand concepts of high-low, loud-soft, and fast-slow.

Concepts

- Rhythm flows on a recurring steady beat. The rhythm of the melody consists of longer and shorter sounds and silences.

- A melody is made up of tones with higher or lower pitches that may change up or down or repeat. When a melody ends on the *home tone* a feeling of repose is created. Visual symbols can be used to show the relationships between tones.

- The basic form in music is the *phrase* or musical thought. Identical phrases contribute to the unity of a composition. A song or other composition may have an *introduction* or a *coda*.

- Songs can be performed with or without accompaniment. Harmony is created when two or more tones are sounded at the same time. Melodies may be combined resulting in a harmonic texture called polyphony.

> **My message to the world is "Let's swing, sing, shout, make noise! Let's not mimic death before our time comes! Let's be wet and noisy."**
>
> —Mel Brooks, interview, <u>New York Times</u>, March 30, 1975

- Sound is produced in diverse ways and can be modified. Tempo is relative rather than absolute. Music can move in a fast or slow tempo. Dynamics in music can be louder or softer. Changes of tempo and dynamics provide a source of variety and expressive meaning in a composition. Characteristic qualities of sounds are determined by the types of voices or instruments which produce them.

- Music has purpose in our everyday life. It comes from all parts of the world.

- Music can be used to express personal feelings on different occasions.

CHAPTER TWO: BRINGING THE CURRICULUM TO LIFE

LESSON PLANNING

Lesson planning is crucial to effectively organize your instruction. Some schools and districts require you to follow the teachers' manuals of commercially prepared textbook series. If your district does not require this, you will be responsible for planning your instructional year. There are as many ways to plan as there are teachers. I don't believe there is any single correct way, and I offer the following suggestions as a guide.

Planning your program of instruction is like planning a dinner party. Before you begin to plan a dinner party, you know certain things. You know how many people you have invited and where you're going to hold the party. You have a certain time frame in mind, and you know that you are going to serve dinner.

First you must decide the presentation of your meal: will it be formal or informal? Sit-down dinner or buffet? Based on that decision you decide what the menu of your meal will be—a traditional favorite or something new? Do you want each food course to be completely different, or do you want the meal to have some unifying elements?

When you know the menu, you collect your recipes to review the ingredients and how to put them together. You schedule your purchases and preparation time. Once the dinner is prepared you assess your results by tasting what you prepare, watching people eat the meal, and seeing what is left over.

Long-Term Planning

You can think of lesson planning in the same way as planning the dinner party. You know how many students you have, you know where you are going to teach them, and you know you are going to teach them the content and skills your school or district requires over the year. You will find this information in your school or district's curriculum guide or course of study. Ask your principal for a copy of the curricular requirements as soon as you can. You know that you need to organize all the information you must teach into a time frame—the school year.

Think about the concepts you want to teach over the next term. Decide what themes (the *presentation* of your school year) will provide good frameworks for these concepts. (Refer to the Using Themes section on page 14 for a discussion of themes.) Choose themes that will interest you and your students—themes that are not too narrow in focus.

Decide what kinds of projects (the *menu*) will give your students many opportunities to learn and practice their learning. Projects can include anything from reading 30 pages in the textbook to converting your classroom into an imaginary rain forest.

Create, select, or choose activities (*recipes*) that will support the themes and promote the learning and practice of skills (*ingredients*).

Before beginning, prepare carefully.
—Cicero

Decide how many days or weeks you will need to accomplish your projects. Make a calendar or time-line of the unit.

Now that you know **what** you want to accomplish you need to plan **how** you will accomplish your long-term plans. Your weekly and daily lesson plans are the way to organize your activities (*recipes*) into a feasible schedule.

A commercially available lesson-plan book will be a useful purchase if your school or district does not provide one. There are many varieties from which to choose, from the most basic notebook-sized with gridded pages to large planbooks that include lesson plan ideas.

Weekly Plans

Make detailed plans and schedule your instruction a week in advance. Include any regular or unusual events in the plan, such as school assemblies, class visitors, library visits, or short school days. Decide what lessons you want to include in the week and fit them into your schedule. The Scheduling section found on page 72 will assist you in deciding when to teach what.

Planning Steps

1. Review the curriculum.

2. Develop an overview of your program of instruction for the year—what concepts you will teach when (as a general idea).

3. Choose themes that provide good frameworks for the concepts.

4. Decide what projects will promote the learning you want to see in the classroom within the theme and across the curriculum.

5. Choose activities to develop the skills that you want to focus on during the thematic unit.

6. Develop a calendar or time-line for the unit.

7. Create your weekly and daily plans.

Daily Plans

For your daily plans you will want to balance activities that require sitting with activities where your students can move around. To begin the year you should assume that 12 to 15 minutes is long enough to require a student to stay focused on the same thing sitting in the same position. As they grow, and you get to know them better, you will find what time frame works for your students. You will also discover exactly what a "wide range of abilities" means. You will have some students who can do whatever you ask them to do, well, in less than half the time that other students require. Plan extension activities or extra projects that will engage these students when they have finished required work. In addition, as you are planning, you may want to decide what homework activities to assign.

Decide what the focus or purpose of the lesson is. It should be clearly stated, because the clearer your purpose, the easier to design a lesson that accomplishes the purpose. Some examples of purposes follow.

- The purpose of this activity is for students to develop and extend original patterns with a variety of manipulative materials.

- The purpose of this activity is to have students pantomime simple antonyms for directional words.

List the materials that will be needed. If you need to order any supplies or get other items, you can do so in advance.

Plan the introduction to your lesson to give students background knowledge that will help them understand the new information. Literature, songs, and pictures can build background knowledge and motivate your students.

Plan exactly what you are going to do and how you are going to do it. Walk through the procedure in your head. If the lesson involves following directions and/or making something, do the activity yourself before you present it to your class. This will help you identify trouble spots. It is much easier to make necessary adjustments before you present it to a group of excited first graders.

After you present the lesson, your students should have time to work independently on the skill you have presented. This gives them the practice necessary to learn it. You may wish to have the students work in small groups.

Planning for Assessment

The final element to consider is how to assess the effectiveness of the lesson. Use informal observations of students involved in the independent activity planned for the lesson combined with formal checks of the work. For more information on record keeping and assessment, see pages 77 and 78.

Thinking through and planning each lesson is essential to your becoming the most effective teacher you can be.

USING THEMES

Themes are big ideas—larger than facts, concepts, or skills. Using a theme allows you to integrate the various content areas. It will provide you with a framework to guide you in the design and development of your instructional program. A theme provides you with a way to make words and abstract ideas concrete and to help your students see how ideas relate to other ideas and to their own experiences. You will find some sample theme lesson plan outlines on pages 51 to 54 and 59 to 61.

Concepts

Language Arts
- Language allows us to express our life experiences and to give names and labels to what we know and value.

Mathematics
- Measurement allows us to attach a number to a quantity using a unit. Selection of the appropriate measuring tool requires considering what will be measured.
- Data can be organized, represented, and summarized in a variety of ways.

Science
- Weather phenomena affect living things.
- Clouds have characteristics by which they can be described.

Health
- Each of us must be prepared to act effectively in times of emergency, including life-threatening situations.

Theme

Weather

Projects
- Read Cloudy with a Chance of Meatballs.
- Choral read April Showers. Create a show for open house.
- Make windmill – observe wind speed.
- Create a weather vane, observe wind direction.
- Explore ice melting.
- Create a temperature graph.
- Create a weather graph with linking cubes.
- Practice emergency drills.
- Talk by city official about how the city handles floods and threats of floods.
- Paint clouds on blue and gray paper.
- Make stuffed cloud hangings.

Skills
- Recite poem. Participate in group activities. Identify and discuss an author's use of word patterns.
- Organize, collect, and interpret data through graphical displays.
- Make observations, gather and interpret data using appropriate tools.
- Compare information and ideas from several different sources. Submit information for class charts, tables, and graphs. Apply information to new situations.

Materials Needed

Windmill worksheet
straight pins
newspaper
White and gray paint
Straws
weather vane worksheet
butcher paper
blue and gray construction paper
thermometers
pencils with erasers (2 for each student)

Literature Needed

Cloudy With a Chance of Meatballs by Judi Barrett (Atheneum, 1978)
April Showers by George Shannon (Greenwillow Books, 1995)
The Air Around Us by Eleonore Schmid (North-South Books, 1992)
The Cloud Book by Tomie de Paola (Scholastic, 1975)

LANGUAGE ARTS

As you plan your language arts program, remember that you can use reading and writing in all curricular areas for assessment purposes. Although language arts processes apply across the curriculum, some specific skills to address in first grade are listed below. They are not listed in any particular order.

- Participate in creating group charts, posters, and stories based on student-selected pictures, filmstrips, or videos.

- Ask questions in complete sentences. Respond appropriately to questions from peers.

- Repeat rhythmic sentences or rhymed couplets read aloud. Read simple verses from class charts.

- Identify and discuss an author's use of special word patterns, phrase patterns, or sentence patterns heard in stories and poetry. Discuss cause and effect.

- Memorize, recite, and illustrate verses from multicultural songs and poems.

- Say or repeat special words, names, greetings, and expressions in several languages. Compare and contrast versions.

- Repeat and respond appropriately to spoken directions.

- Restate directions for participating in a familiar playground activity in sequence.

- Locate books in school and classroom libraries, and discuss uses of primary-level reference materials, including picture dictionaries in different languages.

- Differentiate between fiction and nonfiction. Differentiate among wordless picture books, poetry books, predictable story books, and circular story books.

- Identify major parts of any book (spine, covers, library call numbers; and title, author's and illustrator's names on the cover or on the title page).

- Alphabetize charted names, items, and new vocabulary to the second letter.

- Write [dictate] personal messages in dialogue journals using invented spelling combined with graphics or pictures.

- Use new vocabulary words and phrases stored in word banks or word walls when contributing to written group stories, and when retelling group stories in sequence.

- Use appropriate uppercase and lowercase manuscript forms when writing captions and titles, or when creating signs and posters relating to assignments.

- Identify the beginning, the middle, and the ending parts of stories.

- Use descriptive vocabulary and synonyms for telling about people, places, things, and events discovered in stories.

- Distinguish between fact and fantasy. Discuss which clues help in determining the difference.

- Retell and pantomime the sequence of a predictable story or activity. Discuss how vocabulary words or phrases are used in context. Create a simple story map.

- Identify, match, and pantomime simple antonyms for directional words.

- Begin using the table of contents for locating information in textbooks, in simple reference books, and in student magazines.

- Identify story incidents, characters, and special words or phrases as personal favorites. Tell why they are favorites. Cluster and classify group favorites.

- Recognize and use correct word order in simple sentences. Contribute ideas and new vocabulary to class stories that are predictable or circular.

- Recognize and use correct punctuation, correct usage of common abbreviations, correct usage of compound words, and correct syntax when editing writing efforts for publication.

- Begin transitioning from invented spelling to conventional spelling when editing own and peer-writing efforts for publication.

- Phonics instruction will include blending two to four phonemes (sounds) into recognizable words, segmenting single-syllable words into their components; spelling three to four phoneme short-vowel words.

Establishing Success

First grade is a critical year in the development of language arts skills. To appreciate this, try to imagine a student skipping from kindergarten to second grade, and imagine how much he or she would struggle! Since the skills acquired in the first grade are fundamental to continued achievement, we must promote early success for each student and encourage positive attitudes about reading and writing.

Learning to read and write occurs over time in a series of stages. We need to consider where each student is along this process, and teach him or her accordingly. By way of analogy, consider toddlers learning to walk. They go through different phases such as pushing up with their arms, rolling over, sitting up, crawling, pulling themselves up, and finally, walking. It would do little good to encourage a toddler to walk when he or she hadn't yet begun crawling! As it is when teaching students to read and write, we must be developmentally appropriate in our instruction.

The Reading Developmental Continuum developed in Australia by First Steps identifies six phases students go through in reading.

Phase 1—Role-play Reading

During this phase, students display reading-like behavior and use pictures to construct meaning out of the text. They may even make up their own words to tell the story.

Phase 2—Experimental Reading

Students realize that print carries meaning, and they focus on expressing the meaning rather than reading the words accurately.

Phase 3—Early Reading

Students become confident and see themselves as readers. They are able to retell the content of the book and develop skill in the use of reading strategies.

Phase 4—Transitional Reading

Students construct meaning through their knowledge of text structure, organization, language features, and subjects. They are able to discuss the text's content based upon their own knowledge of the subject.

Phase 5—Independent Reading

Students automatically use a range of reading strategies when constructing meaning from the text. They are able to read fluently while comprehending the material read.

Phase 6—Advanced Reading

Students reflect on the author's position when writing the story, describe the purpose and genre, compare and contrast different points of view, select important or useful information, and ignore irrelevant material.

So how do we promote success for all students during this process? First, we provide a positive environment, a place where mistakes are understood as opportunities for learning, and where all individuals are accepted. Second, we teach language arts concepts through meaningful experiences, examples, and positive daily situations. Finally, we focus more on language content rather than form. Students will learn language form through daily interactions with others around them.

> In teaching it is the method and not the content that is the message—the drawing out, not the pumping in.
> —Ashley Montagu

Reader's Workshop

Let's recall some basic goals for language arts instruction. In addition to developing the necessary skills in each student, we want to instill a love for reading into each child, and help create life-long learners. Incorporating a Reader's Workshop program into your classroom will result in an effective and exciting language-arts curriculum. This program offers students the opportunity for continual success and provides them with a sense of ownership in their learning. Reading becomes both entertaining and rewarding for each student. Too often, children are forced to read material that is developmentally inappropriate, whether too easy or too difficult. The Reader's Workshop approach allows each student to discover his or her current reading level and enjoy success at that level. This program makes learning to read approachable, challenging, and fun for every student in your class, and I strongly recommend it to you.

Allowing Children Choice

To begin this program, you should have a wide variety of literature, ranging in level and topic. If your classroom literature supply is low, send a letter home to parents asking for donations of literature that can be returned to them at the conclusion of the year. Within a few weeks, you might be surprised at the size of your in-class library. An important aspect of the Reader's Workshop program is allowing students choice in the material they read. When given this choice, students are more likely to read outside of school, become independent learners, and value reading.

The first concept you teach your students is that books can be "too easy," "just right," or "too hard." A "too easy" book can be read fluently, without causing hesitations or delays while referring to any particular reading strategies. It might be a book that a student has read before or knows every word of. A "just right" book is read with some difficulty, and the student comprehends the material. A "just right" book will test and expand a student's reading vocabulary. These books are developmentally appropriate, and they allow students to practice using different reading strategies. When a student struggles through many of the words, isn't helped by reading strategies, and has little or no comprehension of what is being read, the book is "too hard." A book that is "too hard" will usually frustrate and discourage the student, often doing more harm than good.

Begin the year by modeling this concept numerous times and allowing the students to practice assessing their own reading by labeling books they read using the "too easy," "just right," and "too hard" terminology. The use of student reading logs (pages 29 and 30) is helpful in teaching this concept. When students can successfully demonstrate an understanding of this concept and can choose books according to their own reading level and interests, they are on their way to becoming independent learners.

Giving Children Time

Along with your normal reading instruction time in the classroom, set aside time each day to allow students to READ! The goal is to provide 30 minutes per day of reading time. This may be a silent reading time or a time in which students share books together. Reading with a partner lets students use their own vocabulary and language skills to think about their reading. During this time, you should model behavior by reading yourself. This might be a great time to read that novel you would otherwise never have time for! The classroom may be the only place where students get uninterrupted reading time, or where they see an adult reading. A few acronyms you can use to identify this time are SSR (Silent Sustained Reading), BEAR (Be Enthusiastic About Reading), or DEAR (Drop Everything And Read).

Developing a Sense of Community and Responsibility in the Classroom

A classroom community is created when all members exist as both learners and teachers. All members work cooperatively, demonstrate respect for one another, encourage one another to do their best, and appreciate individual differences. Each member is given responsibility and challenged with high expectations.

Developing a responsibility chart like the one found in the sidebar gives students clear expectations and allows you to work individually with each student. Recite the chart aloud with the students before each workshop begins. If students get off track during this time, you can remind them of their responsibilities.

Organization

Student's Reading File

Each student gets his or her own Reading File, a hanging file folder placed in an accessible location. Students access their Reading Files whenever materials are needed. These files will greatly increase your level of classroom organization, not to mention the students' organization as well. The Student Reading File contains the following items.

Student Reading Log

Two sample student reading logs are included in this chapter (pages 29 and 30). The first sample includes columns for title and author and allows students to place a check mark in the appropriate category for the book's level. The second sample can be used with more advanced students. It adds an area for writing a short summary, or "gist," of the story. Whichever form you choose, remember that the students fill these out themselves.

"Just Right" Books

The student should keep one or two "just right" books in his or her file for use during individualized conferencing or reading practice.

Story Grammar Charts

Students complete these forms (page 32) to help them think carefully about a book and get organized for a project.

Teacher's Responsibilities

1. Provide materials.
2. Teach mini-lessons.
3. Be helpful to each student.
4. Provide books.
5. Give advice and guidance.

Student's Responsibilities

1. Be a good listener.
2. Don't waste time or bother others.
3. Help each other.
4. Try and try again (ask 3 before me).
5. Be respectful.

Buddy Reading

Looks Like:

Two people sitting side by side

One person reads

One person listens

Book in the middle

Sounds Like:

Quiet reading voices

Listener gives think time or coaching

Listener gives compliments

Projects

Students should use the folders to store current Reader's Workshop projects and associated materials.

Teacher's Reading Record

Create a Reading Record file for each student. Label a manila file folder and fasten 10 Anecdotal Record Sheets (page 28) inside. Use the folder during individual conferences. In the left column of the Anecdotal Record Sheet, note the date, your initials, the title of the book, and, if relevant, the reading level of the book. In the column to the right, record any observable reading behaviors, reading strategies used, and notable areas for improvement. Use a chart to keep track of each individual reading conference (page 34). The chart includes a key to note who reads with the student (you, your aide, or a parent volunteer, for example). A reasonable goal is for each student to read with individual supervision two times per week. The more the better, as the student will improve with every reading opportunity.

Teaching Mini-Lessons

A mini-lesson is essentially a brief period of instruction in which you introduce students to new reading skills and concepts. Use these mini-lessons to explain the differences between "too easy," "just right," and "too hard" books. Reading strategies (page 33) should be taught in mini-lessons as well. Model these strategies to the students at every opportunity.

Buddy Reading

When the students are successfully choosing "just right" books, introduce them to the concept of "buddy reading." A pair of students sit side by side with a book in the middle. One student reads while the other actively listens and coaches. When the student reading gets stuck, the other will ask, "Do you want think time or coaching?" When a student chooses think time, the reading buddy remains silent. This allows the student to think about his or her reading. If the student chooses coaching, the reading buddy offers help using a reading strategy. Model this process a few times before having students practice on their own. It takes time for the students to catch on, but once they do, you will find them buddy-reading during their 30-minute reading time.

At-Home Reading

First graders should spend a good part of every day reading. Reading time during school is essential, but students will always improve more rapidly when reading at home. Send a letter home to parents explaining your homework philosophy, and include an *At-Home Reading Log* (page 31). Students can return these completed forms at the end of each week.

Reader's Workshop Projects

Reader's Workshop projects are miniature book reports created by the student. These projects incorporate literature with art, writing, reading, speaking, and listening. Begin by reading a storybook aloud to your students and discussing the story elements you want to teach (for example, beginning, middle, and ending). Then choose one project, and model how it is made and how it represents the story read. All projects include the title, the author's name, the student's name, the date, and some form of writing.

Story Comprehension Projects

Pop-up Book

Getting Started:

Fold an 8½" x 11" piece of copy paper in half, short end to short end to make a 5½" x 8½" rectangle. Along the folded edge, use a ruler to measure 3¾" inches from the left side, and mark the spot. Then measure and mark one inch from the first mark. At each mark, cut a slit approximately one inch long, so that you have two one-inch parallel slits. (Measurements do not have to be exact.) Fold the tab you have created. Unfold the tab and open the paper. Refold the tab inside the paper, so that it will "pop up" when the book is opened. Make a cover by stapling the copy paper to a sheet of construction paper.

Instructions to Students:

1. Draw characters and objects on the pages or on other pieces of paper and glue them to the book. Drawings glued to the middle section will "pop up" when the book is opened.

2. Use the pop-up book to show one of the following:

   a. problem and solution
   b. a summary of the story
   c. episodes
   d. facts

3. Write about your project on the cover or back of the book.

Triorama

Getting Started:

Begin with a large square piece of white construction paper of any size, and fold in half diagonally from corner to corner twice. Unfold. Cut along one of the four fold lines. Overlap the two flaps that were split by the cut, and staple them together. The students draw the setting and characters inside the triorama and use pieces of construction paper to make pop-up or movable figures.

Instructions to Students:

1. Draw your favorite setting from the story inside the triorama.

2. Create the characters with construction paper and put them inside the setting.

3. Write about the scene you created.

Triorama

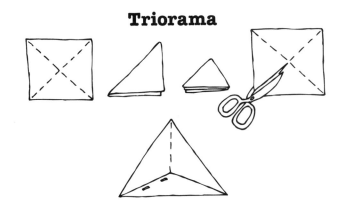

Pop-up Book

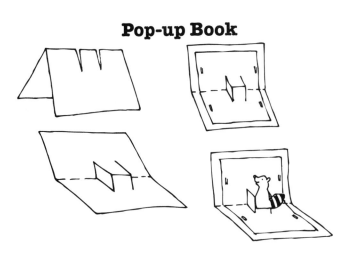

21

Poster

Getting Started:
Provide each student with crayons and a large piece of construction paper.

Instructions to Students:
1. Draw the characters and setting from your favorite part of the story.

2. On the reverse side, write about the scene you drew.

Bookmark

Getting Started:
Provide each student with a light-colored strip of construction paper at least four inches wide and 8 inches long (could be wider and/or shorter or longer) folded in half lengthwise.

Instructions to Students:
1. Fold paper in half lengthwise.

2. Draw the main character at the top of the front page (fold to the left like a book).

2. Cut around the drawing through the front and back pages of the bookmark.

3. Write the title, the author, your name, and the date on the front.

4. Use your bookmark to show one of the following:

   a. characters and their traits

   b. facts

   c. summary of events or individual episodes

5. Write about your project on the inside.

Paper Bag Prop

Getting Started:
Provide each student with a small paper bag, construction paper, and craft sticks.

Instructions to Students:
1. Draw a picture of the setting on the bag, and label the objects in the picture. Also include the title, the author, your name, and the date.

2. Create stick characters (puppets) using construction paper and craft sticks.

3. Store stick characters inside the paper bag, and use them when retelling the story during share circles.

4. On a separate piece of paper, write a summary of the story to put inside the bag.

Bookmark

Poster

Paper Bag Prop

Book Cover

Getting Started:
Provide each student with a large piece of construction paper that has been folded in half widthwise to look like a book.

Instructions to Students:
1. Draw the characters and the setting on the front cover. Include the title, the author, your name, and the date.

2. On the inside left, describe the main character using physical and personality traits.

3. On the inside right, write a summary of the story.

Projects for Learning Character Traits
Character T-shirt

Getting Started:
Provide a T-shirt-shaped piece of construction paper for each student.

Instructions to Students:
1. Draw a picture of the main character and the setting on the front of the shirt.

2. Describe the character on the back of the shirt. Include the title, the author, your name, and the date.

Wanted Poster

Getting Started:
Provide each student with a piece (any size) of white construction paper.

Instructions to Students:
1. Draw a picture of the main character and the setting on the top half of the paper.

2. Write "WANTED" above the picture.

3. Below the picture, describe the character's physical and personality traits.

4. On the back, write a summary of the story.

Book Cover

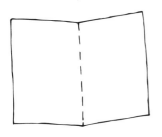

T-shirt

Wanted Poster

Education in the long run is an affair that works itself out between the individual student and his opportunities. Methods of which we talk so much play but a minor part. Offer the opportunities, leave the student to his natural reaction on them, and he will work out his personal destiny, be it a high one or a low one.

—William James, speech, "Stanford's Ideal Destiny," Stanford University, 1906

23

Sequence of Events Projects

Flip Book

Getting Started:

Using two 8½" x 11" sheets of paper, overlap the sheets so that the top sheet is one inch higher than bottom. At approximately the halfway point on the top sheet, fold both pages over onto each other as a unit to create "tabs" of about equal width. Staple the sheets together on the fold.

Instructions to Students:

1. Draw characters and settings on every page to illustrate one of the following sequences:

    a. problem and solution

    b. beginning, middle, and ending

    c. events

    d. fact

2. On each page, describe the illustration.

3. On the cover, include the title, the author, your name, and the date.

Flip Book

Story Map

Getting Started:

Provide a large piece of construction paper for each student.

Instructions to Students:

1. At the top of the paper write the title, the author, your name, and the date.

2. Draw a small picture of each event in the story.

3. Label the characters and setting, and draw arrows indicating the order of events.

4. Write a summary of the story's events on the reverse side.

Story Map

TITLE   AUTHOR   NAME   DATE

> **The object of education is to prepare the young to educate themselves throughout their lives.**
> —Robert Hutchins

Share Circles

At the end of the week, once the students have completed their projects, it is time to share them. Sharing allows the students to celebrate their reading successes, to speak about what they learned from the books they read, to practice listening, to respond with questions and compliments, and to reaffirm their positions in the classroom community.

The students gather in a circle and place their books and projects behind them. Model for the students what a share circle looks and sounds like. The students take turns retelling the "gist," or summary, of their books, talking about the projects they created, and reading what they wrote. Students listening may respond with questions and compliments. Once the students learn how a share circle works, they can conduct them on their own.

Writer's Workshop

Writer's Workshop consists of five basic elements: mini-lessons, independent writing, conferencing, publishing, and author's chair. The purpose of Writer's Workshop is to allow children choice in their writing. Students determine what to write and how long to write. Within this program, it is simply a matter of time before students become self-motivated and want to write more and for different purposes.

Begin by teaching a mini-lesson on a particular skill or writing convention you want the students to learn. After the mini-lesson, the students can begin applying what they learned. When they complete a story, letter, or other writing project, they sign up for a conference with you.

Call each student up one at a time for individual conferences. Start by asking the students to read their material aloud. Keep a positive tone, encouraging them on their accomplishments. Work on areas needing improvements such as spelling or punctuation. Verbally acknowledge areas where the students are performing well, and indicate one aspect of their writing that they can seek to improve when writing their next story.

When finished conferencing, the student's next step is to "publish" his or her work. If you have a computer in the classroom, the stories can be published on the computer. At the beginning of the year, you should write or type the work for the students. By the end of the year, they should be ready to do this on their own. The goal in publishing is to create a visually appealing book that the student will be proud of. Whether you print it out or write it by hand, leave space for the student to illustrate the book.

Reader's Workshop Program

Sample Schedule

Monday—Mini-lesson on a reading strategy, buddy reading, reading logs

Tuesday—Read aloud, model a project, students work independently while you conduct individual conferences

Wednesday—Mini-lesson review of a reading strategy, buddy reading, students work on projects while you conference

Thursday—Review responsibility chart (page 19), students work independently on projects, or read quietly if they are done early, while you conference

Friday—Share circle

Writer's Workshop

- mini-lessons
- independent writing
- conferencing
- publishing
- author's chair

When a book is published and all of the illustrations are added, students are on their way to the "author's chair." First, however, authors must obtain three signatures from classmates who have heard the story read aloud. This process allows students to practice reading the book several times before going to the author's chair.

The author's chair is an opportunity for the students to share their published works with the whole class. They have gone through the writing, editing, and publishing processes and are now ready to share their book with their peers. One student will sit in a chair in the front of the room and read aloud to the class. This is the culminating event in a Writer's Workshop project. After its conclusion, students begin the writing process again with new stories.

Preparing for Writer's Workshop requires minimal effort. You will create handmade books (possibly as simple as blank paper inside a colored cover) to use for publishing each student's writing project. You might also designate Writing Folders for each student and a special place in the classroom where they store their work. Since many first graders are not yet ready to write complete sentences at the beginning of the year, give them blank paper as opposed to lined paper. They can fill the paper with words and illustrations to represent their stories.

Directed Listening and Thinking Activity

This activity is designed to promote listening, thinking, and speaking skills while giving students an opportunity to appreciate literature. When teaching this lesson, avoid using "right" and "wrong" terminology. Always use a positive tone and encourage all students to promote maximum participation. Make sure to set a pace that keeps students focused.

1. Select a storybook with an interesting plot that includes a problem and a solution.

2. Have students view the book's cover and title. Select volunteers to make predictions and discuss what the story could be about.

3. View pictures of the first few pages and ask for predictions.

4. Read several pages aloud to the students. Ask students for a summary of the story's events, and check to see if any predictions came true.

5. Repeat the process until the entire book is read.

TIP!

Publishing student work is an excellent area to use parent volunteer help. Ask a parent to do the word processing for you and the students, or to help students as they learn to use the computer.

Poetry Chart Lessons

Poetry is a valuable tool to use when teaching reading skills. Students enjoy choral reading, singing, or chanting to poetry while learning to read simultaneously. This type of lesson can be done with most poetry, but poems with repetitions and rhyming words are ideal. Here is a sample of a poem that works well for a poetry lesson.

OUT IN THE BARNYARD
sung to "Up on the Housetop"

Out in the barnyard the spider lives.
How much help to the farmer it gives.
Capturing insects that crawl and fly,
Ten, twenty, thirty, forty, fifty, oh my!

Spin, spin, spin, building a web.
Spin, spin, spin, eight busy legs.
Out in the barnyard, looking around.
Capturing insects without a sound.

Materials Needed: butcher paper, different colored markers, a pointer stick, poem, construction paper, scissors, glue, crayons

Activity Description: Begin by copying a poem onto a large piece of butcher paper, leaving room for pictures around the words. Hang the poem up in a visible spot where all students can see it. Read through the poem once, pointing to the words while the students read along silently. As you read the poem a second time, have the students participate. If the poem can be sung to a song, then sing while reading. Once the students are familiar with the poem, you can begin the instructional part of the lesson.

First decide what you are going to teach. Do you want to focus on sight words, picture clues, beginning and ending sounds, or rhyming words? If you are teaching rhyming words, you can ask for student volunteers to point them out. If you are focusing on sight words, then you might ask, "Who can find all the *the* words?"

Finally, have the students make pictures to decorate the poetry chart. Brainstorm with your students what picture clues they can make to decorate the poem, and help them read it. Next, let the students use construction paper, crayons, glue, and scissors to create the picture clues, which they paste to the butcher paper surrounding the words. When the students complete this task, hang the chart in the room for decoration.

Poetry chart lessons can be changed to provide a variety for the students and teach many different skills. You may consider having a poem of the week. Your poem should correlate with whatever subject or theme you are teaching. You can use the poem for poetry chart lessons, handwriting practice, an art activity, singing, choral reading, or role-playing.

Good collections of poetry for children are:

The Random House Book of Poetry for Children (Random House, 1983)

Rhythm Road—Poems to Move To Selected by Lillian Morrison (Lothrop, Lee, & Shepard, 1988)

An interesting resource for using poetry in the classroom is *Pass the Poetry, Please!* by Lee Bennett Hopkins (Harper & Row, 1987)

Consult with your school or local public children's librarian for more poetry ideas.

Anecdotal Record Sheet for _____

Student Name

Date, Initials, Book Title, Reading Level	Observations, Notes

Teacher: Make ten copies of this for the Reading Record file folder you keep for each student.

FS122003 Getting Ready to Teach First Grade

Student Reading Log

Name_____

Title and Author	Too Easy	Just Right	Too Hard
Date:			

Title and Author	Too Easy	Just Right	Too Hard
Date:			

Title and Author	Too Easy	Just Right	Too Hard
Date:			

Title and Author	Too Easy	Just Right	Too Hard
Date:			

Student Reading Log

Name _____ Date _____

Title and Author	Summary (Gist):
Too Easy ☐ **Just Right** ☐ **Too Hard** ☐	

Title and Author	Summary (Gist):
Too Easy ☐ **Just Right** ☐ **Too Hard** ☐	

At-Home Reading Log

Name _____

Week of _____	Book Title	Minutes Read	Adult Signature
Monday			
Tuesday			
Wednesday			
Thursday			
Friday			
Saturday			
Sunday			

Teacher: Make copies of this log sheet for your students to take home and complete with their parents. Have students turn them in every week.

Story Grammar Chart

Name: _____ Date: _____

Title and Author	My Project will be a:
	Poster Wanted Poster Triorama Paper Bag Prop Story Map Book Cover Flip Book Bookmark Pop-up Book Character T-shirt *(Please circle the project you are creating.)*

Character(s)	Summary (Gist)

Setting(s)	

Problem	Solution

©Frank Schaffer Publications, Inc.   **32** reproducible   FS122003 Getting Ready to Teach First Grade

Reading Strategies

 Look at the picture and get your mouth ready to say the word.

 Take a running start. (Try reading the sentence again from the beginning.)

 Skip the word and come back to it.

 Sound it out.

 Break the word into parts.

 Does it make sense? Does it look right? Does it sound right?

 Ask someone.

Individual Conferencing Record

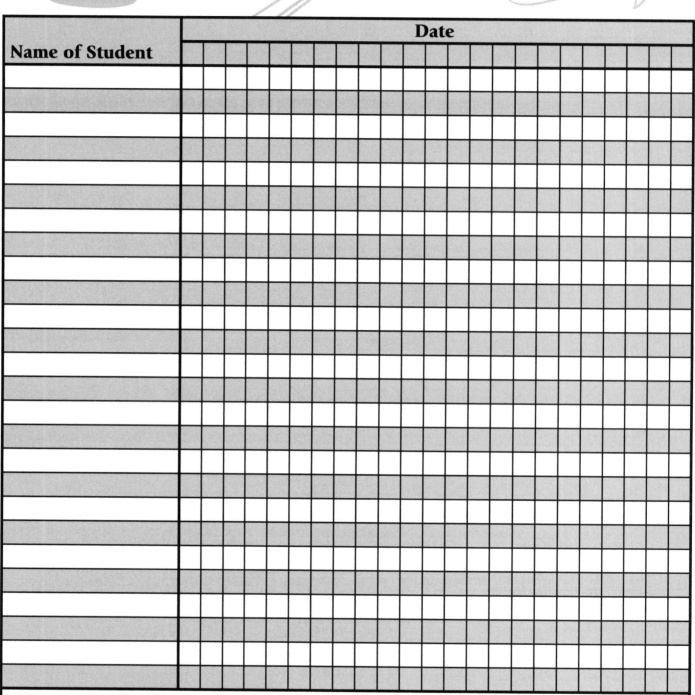

Name of Student	Date																				

Symbols: x = Teacher
+ = Teacher Assistant
0 = Parent Volunteer

Teacher: Use this record sheet to keep track of individual conferences with each student.

MATHEMATICS

- Compare and sort objects by describing similarities, differences, shape, and size.

- Classify objects using shape, size, and other attributes.

- Construct and then describe the properties of the following geometric shapes: circle, square, triangle, and rectangle, and relate them to shapes in the environment.

- Compare and order objects according to their length using terms such as longer and shorter.

- Estimate and measure length in nonstandard units.

- Estimate and measure to the nearest centimeter and meter.

- Estimate and measure length to the nearest inch and foot.

- Compare and order objects according to their weight using terms such as heavier and lighter.

- Estimate and measure weight in nonstandard units.

- Use personal experiences to describe events in sequence. Use terms such as before, after, first, next, and last.

- Read an analog clock to state time on the hour and one-half hour and relate specific times to daily events.

- Name the value of and compare penny, nickel, dime, quarter, half dollar, and dollar.

- Recognize and extend patterns by using concrete materials.

- Predict outcomes and record results of simple probability experiments.

- Organize, collect, and interpret data through graphical displays (concrete, pictorial, and bar graphs).

- Count, read, and write numbers as appropriate to describe and compare quantities.

- Count by twos, fives, and tens to identify number patterns.

- Count backward from 20.

- Use ordinal numbers through tenth to describe position.

- Use concrete materials to discover and describe odd and even numbers.

- Express numbers before, after, and between a given number from 1 to 100.

- Use concrete materials to demonstrate a number that is ten more or ten less than a given number.

- Compare, order, and record number patterns from 1 to 100.

- Use problem-solving strategies to demonstrate understanding of addition and subtraction facts through 18.

- Solve addition and subtraction problems, including money.

- Identify and construct fractional parts of a whole—one-half, one-third, and one-fourth.

- Use the terminology *more, greater than, fewer, less than, same as,* and *equal.*

Math Manipulatives

Teaching mathematics in the first grade requires the use of many different manipulatives, such as play money, place value blocks, counters, mini-clocks, dice, and pattern blocks. Students who are encountering these materials for the first time are often intrigued by them and want to play with them. Before using each set of manipulatives in class for the first time, allow your students to explore them. This way, they won't be as likely to get off task when you begin instruction. If you have your students arranged in cooperative table groups, you can set the manipulatives in the middle of their tables and let the students be creative.

Daily Opening

Students learn math skills through repetition and practice. Unfortunately, simple drills are usually boring and abstract. Our goal is to make math instruction both fun and practical. One of the best ways to accomplish this goal is by incorporating math into a daily opening routine.

Begin by creating an interactive bulletin board in the front of the room, near where you take attendance. This bulletin board includes the following components: a calendar, a row of seven library-book pockets (one for each day of the week), a problem of the day, a weather graph, a classroom-use digital time clock, a standard analog clock (a Judy clock), a magnetic money tray, and three place value cups. On the wall, leave space to construct a number line.

The Calendar

Each day have a different student place a calendar piece on the calendar and tell the class what the date is. For example, *Today is Tuesday, September 7.* In each of the seven library-book pockets, place a number card that corresponds to that day's date. Label the front of the pockets with the days of the week. Also provide taller cards labeled *Yesterday, Today,* and *Tomorrow.* Each day, let a student place these cards in the appropriate pockets, behind the date cards.

Magnetic Money Tray

For this ongoing activity you need a steel cookie sheet and plastic magnet strips. The magnet material is self-adhesive and can be bought in a coil at hardware stores. This is a versatile material for your classroom, because you can cut the magnet into whatever shape you want with regular scissors.

Place magnetic strips on the back of coins and attach them to the cookie sheet. The magnetic money tray can be used in a math center, to make the date in the daily opening, or for teaching students how to count money. This is a hands-on activity that provides a meaningful experience for the students.

Hang the tray from the bulletin board. The student will use the magnetic money pieces to make the date with the money. If the date is the 25th, the student would find all the combinations of coins that result in 25 cents (for example, 1 quarter, 2 dimes and 1 nickel, 25 pennies, and 5 nickels among others).

Velcro® Money Chart

Another option for teaching money and place-value concepts is a Velcro® money chart. You can purchase this chart from a teacher supply store or make your own. The chart can be made out of vinyl, fabric, or posterboard. Using a sewing machine or the adhesive backing, attach five fuzzy Velcro® strips on the chart vertically to make columns. Label the columns *100, 25, 10, 5,* and *1.* Adhere hooked Velcro® strips on the backs of five pennies, two nickels, five dimes, four quarters, and one dollar bill. Place the money in a cup next to the chart.

Have students place a penny on the chart for each day of school. When they get five pennies on the chart, they make a fair trade for a nickel and place it in the *5* column. When they get two nickels, they will make a fair trade for a dime, and so on. Fair trades are always made when a value can be met with a higher coin or dollar bill.

The Number Line

Consider using an expandable number line that can grow with each day of the school year. One cute way of doing this is to draw and cut out the head of a friendly worm and then create numbered segments for each school day. Attach the head to the wall. Then as students take turns adding a number to "Dr. Worm" each day, they can practice counting by twos, fives, and tens. For example, on the 25th day of school, they can count by fives, on the 50th day of school, they can count by tens. Dr. Worm, or any number line, is also an effective tool for teaching the concept of odd and even.

The Weather Graph

Create a weather key with symbols to represent the type of weather common in your area. Use linking cubes to represent the kind of weather for the day. If it is cloudy, use a blue linking cube. If it is sunny, use a yellow linking cube. Each day a student can decide what the weather is and place a linking cube in a cup. At the end of the month, you can create a graph representing the weather pattern for the month.

- The elementary school years are crucial in a child's cognitive and affective development, and you are the central figure. You structure classroom experiences to implement the curriculum and create a supportive environment for learning to take place. In most activities, you are the guide, the coach, the facilitator, and the instigator of mathematical explorations.

- You give children the gift of self-confidence. Through your careful grouping, astute questions, appropriate tasks, and realistic expectations, each student can experience success.

- Long after they forget childhood events, your students will remember you. Your excitement and interest permeate the room and stimulate their appreciation for mathematics.

- Through your classroom practices, you promote mathematical thinking, reasoning, and understanding.

- You lay the foundation on which further study takes place. You give students multiple strategies and tools to solve problems. The questions you ask and the problems you pose can capture your students' imagination, arouse their curiosity, and encourage their creativity.

- You facilitate the building of their knowledge by giving them interesting problems to solve, which leads to the development of concepts and important mathematical ideas.

- Rules, algorithms, and formulas emerge from student explorations guided by you, the teacher of mathematics.

—Miriam A. Leiva, <u>Curriculum and Evaluation Standards for School Mathematics, Addenda Series</u>

37

The Problem of the Day

Using magnetic numbers or a chalkboard, make a problem of the day. Include addition and subtraction problems, place value blocks, and word problems. Students can solve the problem on their own, as a whole group, or allow a designated helper for the day to try to solve it.

The Digital and Analog Clocks

Make a set of small cards with a different time word on each card (example: *four o'clock*). Have students take turns selecting a card, reading the words aloud, and showing the card to the class. Then let the student make the digital clock and analog clock represent the time shown on the card.

Place Value

Teach place value in your daily opening using objects such as beans, straws, toothpicks, and pipe cleaners. For each day of school you add one of the objects to a cup. Label three cups as *Ones*, *Tens*, and *Hundreds*. You might even have fun with it and label the cups with names such as *Hoola-Hoopy's Ones Place*, *Scooby-Dooby's Tens Place*, and *Mickey Moose's Hundreds Place*. Be creative and have fun.

"I wonder why . . .?"

"What would happen if . . .?"

"Tell me about your pattern."

"Can you do it another way?"

"Our group has a different solution."

These inviting words give students the freedom to be creative, the confidence to solve problems, and the power to do mathematics. When you give your students the opportunity to construct their own knowledge, you are opening the doors of mathematics to all young learners.

This is the challenge. This is the vision.

—Miriam A. Leiva, <u>Curriculum and Evaluation Standards for School Mathematics, Addenda Series</u>

More Math Activities

There are several important math tools you should put on the wall and use during math lessons and any other math moments you find during the day. Every classroom should have a number line with positive numbers that go at least as far as 100, and a number chart with numbers 1 to 100.

Place Value Activities

Beyond your daily opening, you can teach place value using other enjoyable activities. A sample place value chart useful for these activities is on page 43. Make as many copies as needed for each student in your class. Then attach each chart to a piece of construction paper and laminate.

Race to a Flat

Materials Needed: dice, place value charts on page 43, place value blocks

Activity Description:

Students get into groups of two to four. Each student is given a place value chart and each group is given a set of place value blocks and two dice. Students sit in a circle and take turns rolling the dice. If, for example, a student rolls a total of 8, he or she counts out 8 ones-blocks and places them in the ones column of the chart. If on the student's next turn, the dice total 5, he or she counts out 5 ones-blocks and puts them with the 8 blocks already on the chart. Now there are 13 ones blocks, and a "fair trade" can be made by exchanging 10 ones-blocks for 1 ten-stick. The ten-stick is put in the tens column on the chart. Now the student has 1 ten-stick and 3 ones-blocks. The game continues until one student accumulates 10 tens-sticks and makes a "fair trade" for 1 hundreds-flat. The student who reaches the flat first wins.

Race to Zero

Materials Needed: dice, place value charts (page 43), place value blocks

Activity Description:

This activity is similar to "Race to a Flat" but different in that the students begin with a flat and race to zero. This teaches the concept of borrowing and is recommended for the advanced students at the end of the year who are developmentally ready to learn this concept.

Students sit in cooperative groups of two to four members. Each student begins with 1 hundreds-flat on his or her place value chart. Students take turns rolling the dice. If a student rolls a 10, he or she trades in the flat for 10 tens-sticks, and trades 1 ten-stick in for 10 ones-blocks. The ones-blocks can then be removed from the place value chart, leaving 9 tens sticks, or 90. It is important that the students go through the process of converting to ones-blocks in order to learn the concept of borrowing. Eventually you can have the students write the symbols on paper while they play the game. The student who reaches zero first wins.

Copy Me

Materials Needed: pencils, paper, place value charts (page 43), place value blocks

Activity Description:

Divide students into pairs. The first student will have a pencil and a piece of paper, and the second student will have a place value chart and a set of place value blocks. The first student writes a number on paper. The second student builds the number with the blocks on the place value chart. The students take turns being the writer and the builder. Partners can challenge each other by writing three-digit numbers.

Individual Math Packets

Individualizing a math program can be very challenging. Students are always working at different levels and speeds. How do we compensate for this? One method is to make an individual math packet for each student in your class. After completing your beginning-of-the-year assessments, you will have a better indication of where your students are at academically. Most first graders need significant amounts of practice with addition and subtraction skills. Using math packets allows the students to work individually and challenge themselves. While students are working through their packets, you have time to conference with small groups or individuals on specific concepts or skills where they need assistance. In creating these packets, remember that students need variety and challenge. Avoid using all addition equations or all subtraction equations. Provide your students with opportunities to think.

Math Story Settings

Story settings are effective tools to use when teaching addition and subtraction skills. They offer students the opportunity to work with manipulatives to understand math concepts. Why does 2 + 2 = 4? Incorporate story settings into the math packets, and have students create their own equations and solve them. Students use counters on their story settings to represent objects being used in the equations. These counters help students explore equations and solutions in concrete ways. I have included one story setting you can copy for your students on page 42. As students have experience with this activity they should draw their own math story settings.

Here is one example. Five dinosaur counters are placed in the lake pictured on the story setting page. Students act out the story as you tell it, and then solve the problem.

There are five dinosaurs swimming in a lake. Two decide to take a walk. How many dinosaurs are left swimming in the lake?

Prove It

In addition to math skills, we also want to develop effective problem-solving skills in our students. We don't just want the answer, we want to know how they got the answer and if there is another way to come up with the same answer. To encourage problem-solving skills, I often ask my students to "prove it," or explain how they reached an answer. This open-ended question forces the students to think about their own thought processes and often results in some very creative responses.

The 100-Inch Worm

Divide the class into groups of four or five students. Give each group a large piece of white butcher paper (not 100 inches long), two or three rulers, crayons, and scissors. Tell your students that they are to create a 100-inch worm that must be at least a foot wide. Show them the materials they will use, and let them begin the activity. The purpose of this lesson is to allow the students to use their problem-solving skills in cooperative groups. Therefore, keep your directions and instruction to a minimum.

Pattern Block Fun

Divide your class into pairs of students. Give each set of partners a plastic bag of pattern blocks and a folder. There should be two of each block in the bag. Each student gets one set of pattern blocks. The folder is opened and stood on end between the partners so that they are unable to see each other's workspace. One student (the designer) arranges his or her blocks to form a design. Then the designer explains to his or her partner how the blocks are arranged. The partner listens to the directions and tries to arrange his or her blocks to match those of the designer. This lesson develops communication, listening, geometric identification, and following directions.

Roll the Dice

Divide your class into groups of two to four students. Give each group two dice, paper, and pencils. The students take turns rolling their dice and marking on paper the number rolled by adding the two numbers shown on the dice. Each time a student rolls, he or she will add the number shown on the dice to the number on his or her paper. The goal is to reach 50 first.

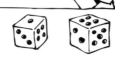

Find the Secret Number

Divide your class into groups of four to six students. Give each group a number line. One player chooses a number on the number line. The other players ask questions to find the secret number. Questions may only be answered using "yes" or "no." The player who guesses the number gets to start a new round by picking a new number.

Class Store

Setting up a class store to teach the concept of money is a meaningful learning experience for students. Purchase or have parents donate items to sell in your store. You can use stickers, pencils, toy cars, bookmarks, and erasers. Students earn play money by following rules, giving compliments, helping classmates, and other positive behaviors. Set up a special place in the classroom for the students to store their money. You can use pencil boxes, pocket charts, or small piggy banks. Open the store once every one or two weeks, and allow two or three students to shop at a time. Make sure it is during a time when the class is busy working on another activity. You will also discover what an effective classroom management tool this can be!

> **If we value independence, if we are disturbed by the growing conformity of knowledge, of values, of attitudes, which our present system induces, then we may wish to set up conditions of learning which make for uniqueness, for self-direction, and for self-initiated learning.**
>
> —Carl R. Rogers, <u>On Becoming a Person</u>, 1961

Number Chart

Use a wall number chart of numbers 1 to 100 to practice skip-counting patterns of twos, fives, and tens. Introduce skip counting by threes, fours, eights, and nines using the chart. If your chart is laminated, write on it with a non-permanent marker to indicate which numbers will be counted in the skip-counting pattern you have chosen. See if your students notice any visual patterns to the skip counting.

Make multiple copies for each student of the Number Chart 1–100 worksheet (page 44).

Use the number chart to guide students to find all the numbers that end in zero, three, or one. What patterns do the students recognize?

Guide students to explore skip-counting patterns on their charts. The students will begin to recognize other patterns independently. As their thinking develops, students can follow other patterns using numbers. One activity would be to color every third number (3, 6, 9, 12, and so on) and have students practice skip counting by threes. What do they notice about the pattern?

Hand out copies of the number chart with missing numbers (cover some of the numbers before you photocopy it). Have students fill in the missing numbers. Discuss the ways they can figure out the missing numbers such as counting, looking at visual patterns on the chart, or comparing it to a complete hundred chart.

As their number sense develops you can cut the complete number chart into sections like puzzle pieces. Have students put the puzzle together. Give them charts to make their own puzzles. An extension of this activity is to use the Number Chart 1–100 with some numbers blanked. Cut the chart into puzzle pieces for students to assemble. They will have to complete number patterns to assemble the puzzle correctly. Eventually you will be able to provide a jigsaw piece of the chart with only one number on it, and your students will be able to complete the missing numbers correctly.

MATH STORY SETTING

Teacher: Make copies of this math story setting for your students. Have them invent math stories based on the setting and using math counters. After they have practiced telling math stories, have them tell math stories and write the equations onto a separate sheet of paper. Refer to page 40 for more information.

FS122003 Getting Ready to Teach First Grade

Place Value Chart

Hundreds 100s	Tens 10s	Ones 1s

Instructions for this chart are on pages 38 and 39.

Number Chart 1–100

 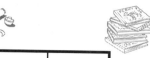

1	2	3	4	5	6	7	8	9	10
11	12	13	14	15	16	17	18	19	20
21	22	23	24	25	26	27	28	29	30
31	32	33	34	35	36	37	38	39	40
41	42	43	44	45	46	47	48	49	50
51	52	53	54	55	56	57	58	59	60
61	62	63	64	65	66	67	68	69	70
71	72	73	74	75	76	77	78	79	80
81	82	83	84	85	86	87	88	89	90
91	92	93	94	95	96	97	98	99	100

FS122003 Getting Ready to Teach First Grade

PHYSICAL EDUCATION

Skills

The activities presented should help students develop their skills as they are growing and changing. There should be a mix of partner and cooperative games to help the students learn to work together and have fun doing it. Physical education and other areas of the curriculum can be integrated to support the various learning styles of your students.

- **Locomotor**—walk in a crossover pattern for 10 feet; run in tag games; begin to run in a relay; perform the basic moves of Hopscotch and Beanbag Hop; perform controlled kick of a beanbag; jump, making a quarter turn; practice jumping with a short jump rope; skip to a simple rhythm; skip to music; leap over a two-foot space; leap to a regular drumbeat; attempt to gallop with the non-dominant foot leading; slide sideward in both directions; start and stop walking on a signal; change directions easily.

- **Non-locomotor**—stretch body parts while sitting and standing; raise the head while lying down.

- **Manipulative movements**—grasp and release the bars, using several grips on the apparatus; throw a yarn ball and hit a target; throw a ball into the air with one hand; throw a ball overhand at a target; attempt to throw a ball with the opposite foot forward; throw a ball to get an out in kickball; catch a beanbag 10 times; bounce a ball 10 times; catch a rolling ball; practice moving to catch a ball; strike two rhythm sticks together to create a rhythm; bounce a ball while walking.

- **Perceptual motor**—identify many body parts such as: eyes, ears, hands, fingers, elbows, and knees; identify the right and left side of one's own body; move to simple oral directions; listen and try to repeat a sequence of movements on command.

- **Flexibility and agility**—crawl and walk over, under, and through obstacles on the floor; perform a few stunts on the apparatus; do a crab walk, bear walk, seal crawl, and inchworm walk.

- **Muscular strength and endurance**—practice the fundamentals of hanging and climbing activities; perform stunts on the horizontal ladder.

- **Cardio-respiratory endurance**—perform locomotor skills for increasing periods of time; follow a simple zig-zag course by running, jumping, and dodging around obstacles such as rubber cones; jog for one to two minutes; jump over a rope held at various low heights.

- **Balance**—Balance on one, two, three, and four parts of the body; move around in a circle while balancing on tiptoes; balance on one foot with eyes closed; walk a line forward, heel to toe, for five feet; walk a line backward, toe to heel.

- **Body awareness (self-image enhancement)**—perform a variety of activities in horizontal and vertical positions; point to the body parts such as chin, knee, and elbow; move in a small group without touching; move fast and then slow; change directions quickly.

- **Self-realization (self-image enhancement)**—begin to develop the concept of setting goals; understand the concept of successful personal performance; realize that practice may be necessary to attain goals.

- **Self-expression (self-image enhancement)**—bend the body slowly in as many ways as possible; exhibit feelings and emotions through movement; attempt to move to the rhythm of a poem.

- **Social behavior**—participate actively in rhythms and games; practice good sportsmanship; participate in decision-making; give best effort; encourage others.

Commands, Attention-Getting Devices, and Formations

When students are performing physical activities, it can be hard to manage your class. If you make your commands and attention-getters fun, they are more likely to be effective. Here are some examples:

Commands

Potato = Sit down

Celery = Stand up

Banana = Spread out

Grapes = Clump together in front of the teacher

Kumquats = Partner up

Attention-Getting Devices

Teacher	Students
"Are you ready?"	"You Bet!"
"Where am I?"	"Here I am!"

Formations

First-grade students often have difficulty forming partners or groups. Here are some different ideas that will help students form groups quickly without getting upset or taking too much time.

Popcorn—Students jump around like popcorn and stick to someone.

X's and O's—Label students with either an *X* or an *O*. Call all X's to one place and all O's to another.

Birthdays—Have students form teams according to their month of birth. Use three months per team when forming four teams and six months per team when forming two teams.

Look at Your Fingernails—After students respond to this command, separate them according to whether their palms are facing up or facing down.

Physical Education Activities

No Touch

This game requires a small, confined area that allows minimum movement. The object of the game is to move around the area without touching anyone. The teacher calls out commands and the students move accordingly while trying to avoid their classmates. Movements might include walking, jogging, running, skipping, jumping, and crawling. When you want the students to stop, yell commands such as "Back to back," "Toe to toe," or "Knee to knee." To challenge the students, you can yell out math problems and have the students get into groups the size of the answer.

I See

You say, "I see." Students respond, "What do you see?" You answer, "I see everyone… (walking, hopping, skipping, doing push-ups, doing sit-ups)."

Shipwreck

Begin by placing signs on the walls of the classroom or gym that designate the ends or sides of a ship—bow (front), port (left), starboard (right), and stern (rear). Then call out different areas of the ship and have students run, jog, skip, and hop to them. When students are familiar with the game, you can challenge them with other commands. For example, you can yell "Shark!" and have students run to the middle of the ship and put their hands over their heads. Or shout "Abandon Ship!" and have students get partners, sit with their feet together, hold hands, and rock back and forth. If you say "Person Overboard!," direct students to find a partner. Have one student get on his or her hands and knees and the partner put one foot up on his or her back and look out. If you yell out "Mates in the Galley!," have students sit with four in a group and hold hands. Finally, if you shout "Pump Out the Water!," have the students do push-ups.

Tag Games

When playing tag, make sure the students know their boundaries.

Walking Tag

Partners take turns chasing each other.

Freeze Tag

When tagged, players stay in their places until they unfreeze by doing five jumping jacks or sit-ups.

Escape Tag

Players must move in a certain way (for example, by plugging their noses or shaking their hips) to prevent being tagged.

Beanbag Tag

Players toss beanbags at people's feet. When a player gets hit, he or she picks up the beanbag and tosses it at someone's feet.

Opposites

For this exercise in antonyms, begin by directing students to do the opposite of what you command. For example, if you say "Run!" the students walk; if you say "Go left!" the students turn right. Other commands you could use include stand tall, hop on your left leg, step backward, smile, and look to your right. Your first graders will enjoy this opportunity to disobey you!

Crab Soccer

To play this game, you will need four markers (orange cones) and a soft, large ball. Set up the four cones to form a small square. Organize the students into four teams, and have them remove their shoes and sit around the edges of the square. Next, give a number to each student by counting off the members of each team. Each student should have a correspondingly numbered classmate on each of the other three teams. If one or more teams is short a player, give one of the players on the team a second number.

Begin play by calling out a number and having the four students with that number crab-walk to the middle of the square and try to kick the ball with their feet. Their goal is to kick the ball across the edge of the square they are facing. The students sitting on the edge defend it by kicking the ball back to the middle of the square. If the ball is kicked over an edge, that defending team gets a point. Teams try to avoid getting points, because the team with the least amount of points wins. Call out new numbers after each score or after a set amount of time. Play this game indoors and avoid grass stains!

47

Basketball Warmups

Provide each student with a basketball. Give them the following directions, and lots of time to explore the motions.

- Jog around the ball.

- Sit on the floor, and roll the ball up and down your body.

- Toss the ball into the air, and catch it with your fingertips.

- Toss the ball back and forth between your hands.

- Pass the ball in a circle around your knees.

- Walk in a figure-eight pattern while dribbling (bouncing) the ball.

- Sit on your knees and dribble the ball using both hands.

- Stand up and dribble the ball.

- Pass the ball under one leg while dribbling.

- Turn your body in a circle while dribbling.

- Hop on both feet and dribble.

- Walk in a circle while dribbling the ball in one spot.

Soccer Warmups

Provide each student with a soccer ball. Give them the following directions, and lots of time to explore the motions.

- Put one foot on the ball and hop around it.

- Jump and tap the ball.

- Drop the ball, let it bounce once, and then trap it.

- Toss the ball up, let it bounce once, and then trap it.

- Roll the ball and walk beside it.

- Dribble (kick) the ball up and down the court.

- Dribble in a figure eight.

- Tap the ball and creep it backward, forward, and sideways.

- Dribble the ball and stop at each line or cone.

Parachute Activities

Clock Walk
Have students hold the parachute with their left or right hands and walk, hop, skip, gallop, or run to make the parachute turn.

Making Waves
Have students, working in groups, take turns lifting their sides of the parachute to "make waves."

Circle the Ball
Place a ball on the raised chute. Have students work together to make the ball roll around the chute. Add another ball to increase the fun.

Popcorn
Place small balls or beanbags on the parachute. Let students shake the chute to make them bounce like popcorn.

Mushroom
Direct students to raise the chute above their heads, walk forward, and then lower the chute behind their backs as they squat down. When this activity is done correctly, the parachute should hold the air inside itself, creating a mushroom-shaped roof over the students' heads. The students may or may not sit inside on the edge of the parachute. If they do sit, make it into an amusement ride by letting students rock forward, backward, and sideways.

Running Number Game
Begin by having the students count off by fours. Then have them run while holding the parachute in one hand. Call out one of the numbers. Direct the students with that number to immediately release their grip on the chute and run forward to the next vacated place. This means they need to run faster than the rest of the class.

SCIENCE AND HEALTH

Science

The goal of science education is that students develop observational skills and learn about life through science. The activities that the students participate in should include classification, observing using the five senses, and designing and testing hypotheses. You act as a guide and allow students to explore and discover on their own.

Skills

- Use a combination of senses to explore and classify objects or events.

- Ask relevant questions concerning natural phenomena.

- Design a simple investigation to illustrate and verify an idea.

- Identify and compare basic characteristics when recording observations of objects and events.

- Compare relative weights and distances related to science activities.

- Generate data by investigating; record data by writing and/or by drawing pictures; and organize data by grouping or sequencing information.

- Suggest possible reasons why and how events take place.

- Analyze and describe data to explain how a situation or event occurred.

- Select and manipulate science materials and equipment in a safe manner.

- Follow directions and safety procedures in pursuing classroom investigations.

- Handle classroom animals in a humane, careful, and safe manner.

- Provide and maintain an appropriate environment for living things.

- Utilize appropriate reading and language skills in comprehending science content.

- Develop and use a science vocabulary.

Health

Skills

- Become aware of personal appearance and neatness.

- Identify personal health practices that protect the health of self and others.

- Tell the difference between being ill and being well.

- Take an active and regular part in physical activities.

- Practice health habits that contribute to good posture.

- Talk about and practice relaxing activities.

- Identify good dental habits.

- Compare ways in which disabled people are similar to non-disabled people.

- Talk about ways to protect vision and hearing.

- Explain why regular health check-ups are important.

Be true to your teeth, and they won't be false to you.

—Soupy Sales

- Describe the role of families in nurturing and protecting its members.

- Explain the function of a family.

- Discuss different types of families—how families are alike and different.

- Discuss ways to cooperate at school and at home.

- Identify signs of one's personal growth.

- Compare and contrast how people and animals parent their young.

- Identify how individuals can assume responsibility for personal health.

- Compare and contrast various types of health care services, including the school nurse.

- Discuss what germs are, and how disease is spread.

- Differentiate between good and bad touching.

- Identify and practice good safety procedures when traveling to and from school.

- Demonstrate appropriate behavior during emergency drills.

- Observe safety rules for the playground.

- Discuss what to do in case of an accident.

KWL Chart

Many science, other curricular areas, and thematic units get a strong start with the use of a KWL chart. KWL stands for Know, Wonder, and Learned. It is an efficient way to introduce a unit. It gives you a good idea of what students already know about an idea, and therefore what information they still need, and what might pique their curiosity.

Take one large piece of butcher paper and divide it into three sections, labeling the separate sections **Know**, **Wonder**, or **Learned**, in that order from left to right, or use three sheets of easel paper, each labeled individually **K**now, **W**onder, or **L**earned.

First ask students what they know about a subject. Write down all the answers—even if what they "know" is incorrect.

Ask them what questions they have about the subject and write their questions in the Wonder section of the chart. You may find that filling in both the **K**now and **W**onder sections simultaneously keeps the momentum of the discussion going well.

Leave the Learned section blank during the introduction phase of the unit. Keep the KWL chart(s) posted during the unit. Add to the Learned section as you finish different lessons, or as students make important discoveries.

Know	Wonder	Learned
Butterflies are pretty. Butterflies fly. They eat leaves. They live in the garden.	Where do they go in the winter? What does a baby butterfly look like?	

Help students develop experiments that will allow them to discover the answers to their questions. When you have finished the topic, review the **L**earned section and add any important conclusions students reach.

Thematic Unit Integration

Ordinarily, science and health curriculum components are structured around textbooks and other materials dedicated to a particular subject. Since first-grade students are still developing basic reading skills, these materials are often inappropriate. This is not to say that science, health, and similar subjects cannot be introduced to first graders in a meaningful way. By using a thematic approach, teachers can generate students' interest and effectively teach these otherwise-challenging subject areas.

A thematic unit takes a single topic and integrates it throughout the curriculum. Topics can include concrete phenomena, literary forms and structure, and other concepts. In science and health, fundamental concepts such as sensory perception, nutrition, and the process of growth or change are popular. The following examples implement activities from a single topic within a thematic unit to teach science and health concepts. While these are not complete units, they should be helpful ideas for you.

Science and Health Unit

Example 1: Weather

Reading/Writing

Read aloud the book *Cloudy With a Chance of Meatballs* by Judi Barrett (Atheneum, 1978). Have students illustrate their favorite parts of the story. Then have them write a few sentences explaining their choices.

Math

Keep a monthly record of the weather patterns using symbols on a calendar. At the end of the month, tally your results and create a bar graph. Ask questions such as *Which weather pattern occurred the most? Which weather pattern happened the least amount of times? How many more days did it rain than snow?*

Science

Give each student an ice cube. Tell your students you are going to have a contest to see who can

make his or her ice cube disappear the fastest. Give the command for them to begin. When a few students are done, bring the class together to discuss how the students tried to make their ice cubes melt. Ask questions such as *How did your ice cube change? What made it change? How could we have made it disappear faster?* Relate this activity to how water and weather change (for example, how snow melts because of the sun's heat).

Art

Create a weather vane and a windmill with your students using the templates on pages 55 and 56. Have students decorate the patterns and cut them out. Attach them to pencils or straws with a pin. Take students outside on a windy day to observe how these instruments work. The students will see how the weather vane indicates the direction of the wind and how the windmill indicates the speed of the wind.

> The world looks so different after learning science. For example, trees are made of air, primarily. When they are burned, they go back to air, and in the flaming heat is released the flaming heat of the sun which was bound in to convert the air into tree. [A]nd in the ash is the small remnant of the part which did not come from air, that came from the solid earth, instead.
>
> These are beautiful things, and the content of science is wonderfully full of them. They are very inspiring, and they can be used to inspire others.
>
> —Richard Feynman

> **Every child should have mudpies, grasshoppers, waterbugs, tadpoles, frogs, mud turtles, elderberries, wild strawberries, acorns, chestnuts, trees to climb, animals to pet, hay fields, pinecones, rocks to roll, sand, snakes, huckleberries and hornets—and any child who has been deprived of these has been deprived of the best part of his education.**
>
> —Luther Burbank

Science and Health Unit

Example 2: *The Very Hungry Caterpillar* by Eric Carle (Philomel, 1987)

This thematic unit ties in to a "Living Things" theme while incorporating the life cycle of a butterfly. Relating literature to science always inspires children and motivates them in their learning.

Reading

Read *The Very Hungry Caterpillar* by Eric Carle (Philomel, 1987) to students with expression and enthusiasm. When you have finished reading, brainstorm with your students a list of favorite foods they would eat if they were the very hungry caterpillar. Write their suggestions on chart paper.

Writing

Create a page for each student with this saying at the top: "If I were the Very Hungry Caterpillar, I would eat …" Leave blank lines for the students to write on. At the bottom of the paper, leave space for the students to draw a picture. These pictures can be displayed in the classroom. You may even want to create a caterpillar with the pictures. You can do this by gluing the pictures onto pieces of round construction paper and overlapping the circles as you hang them on the wall. Make sure to create some kind of head for the caterpillar.

Math/Art

You can teach the concept of symmetry with butterflies. Collect pictures of different butterflies and allow the students to observe the patterns on the wings. Point out how they are symmetrical, the same on each wing. Using the butterfly design on page 57, the students can create their own designs and practice symmetry. Students may use tissue paper, markers, and crayons to design the patterns on their butterflies.

Science

Make this unit meaningful for the students by bringing real caterpillars into the classroom. Consult a reference, such as *How to Raise Butterflies* by E. Jaediker Norsgaard (Dodd, Mead, 1988), for details on how to prepare and maintain a suitable habitat for caterpillars. Allow students to observe the caterpillars and record their observations in a journal. They can make predictions or hypotheses regarding what they think will happen to the caterpillars or how they will change. Set aside time daily for the students to observe the caterpillars and record changes. They may want to change their predictions as time goes by. When the caterpillars turn into butterflies, have a celebration and let the butterflies go outside.

Give the students mealworms or moths to observe. Have the students observe them and record their observations. Then compare these creatures to the caterpillars. Make a Venn diagram with your students, and allow them to brainstorm similarities and differences.

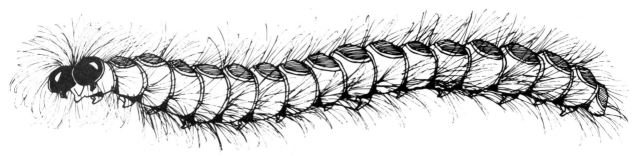

Science and Health Unit

Example 3: My Five Senses

Writing

Create a book for your students to complete using clip art and borders. Each page of the book should be dedicated to a different sense. The headings on the pages could include the following:

These are my favorite things to see.
These are the sounds I like to hear.
These are the foods I love to taste.
These are some of my favorite things to smell.
These are things I enjoy touching.

Depending on the developmental levels of the students, they can write about these things or draw pictures. Staple the pages together, and allow students time to share their books with classmates.

Science/Health

As a whole group, practice identifying the five senses. Read the following sentences to your class. Let the students decide which sense they would use to know these things:

Bread is baking in the oven.
A stove is hot.
Candy is sweet.
A fire truck is coming.
Your sweater has stripes.
A cat's fur is soft.
Mom washed the floor.
Ice cubes are cold.
Mrs. Workman has an announcement.
The buses are here.
It's time to clean up and move to a new center.
There is a skunk on the road.
It is time to line up outside.

Listening

Take your students for a trip around the school. Take them to the office, the gym, the music room, the library, the playground, the classroom, or any other place in your school. While visiting these places, have the students practice listening to the sounds they hear. Remind them not to disturb anyone while they are visiting. When you return to the classroom, brainstorm and make a list of all the sounds they heard while visiting different rooms and locations.

Fill four or five canisters with different objects that make noise. Fill another set of canisters with the same objects. The objects could include such things as rice, beans, dice, rocks, counters, chalk, and sand. Put the canisters in a center. The students will practice shaking the canisters and matching up the sounds that are the same. When a student has them all matched, he or she can look inside and see if his or her guesses were correct.

Tasting

Bring in different food items for the students to taste. You may want to bring in things that are sour, sweet, salty, and bitter. Foods might include lemons, sugar, pretzels, and bitter chocolate. Let the students take turns tasting each item. Then have them write about how each one tasted. Introduce the students to the words *sour*, *sweet*, *salty*, and *bitter*.

Imagination is more important than knowledge.

—Albert Einstein, <u>On Science</u>

Smelling

In different jars, cans, or bottles, that cannot be seen through, put vinegar, chocolate, pickles, vanilla, hot sauce, cinnamon, peanut butter, perfume, maple syrup, and mouthwash. Label each jar with a number and keep a key for yourself. Divide your class into cooperative groups. Give each group a piece of paper with the numbers 1 to 10. Let the students take turns smelling each jar. Then have them decide as a group if they think it smells good or bad. If they agree that it smells bad, they draw a picture of an unhappy face next to the number of that jar on the paper. Then they will try to guess what they are smelling and write their guess next to the happy or unhappy face. When everyone is done smelling the jars, you can go through each jar and let the students tell you what they thought it was. Using your key, you can tell them what items are in each jar. Put these items in a center for another time.

Science and Health Unit

Example 4: Nutrition

Science

Introduce the five basic food groups: Grains, Vegetables, Fruit, Meat, and Dairy Products. Let the students brainstorm lists of foods that belong in each food group. Chart their ideas on butcher paper. Have each student make a list of the foods he or she ate for lunch and determine which food groups were included in the meal and which, if any, were missing. Ask what the students could eat to make a healthier lunch.

Poetry/Reading

Here is another example of a poem you can use for a poetry chart lesson (see page 27).

Five food groups for us to eat—
Vegetables, Dairy, Fruit, and Meat.
Don't forget to eat Grain,
It gives you energy for your brain.
Five food groups for you and me,
They help us to stay healthy.
Five food groups for you and me,
Eat a wide variety.

Math

Ask each student to bring a recipe from home, preferably one that is nutritious and uses whole numbers (for example: 1 cup). Teach students how to double a recipe. Allow them to practice this concept by doubling their own recipes.

Cut several coupons from the newspaper or magazines. You may want to laminate them for future use. Give each student a coupon and some play money. Have the students practice making the amount shown on the coupon with the coins. When they finish, they can switch coupons with a partner.

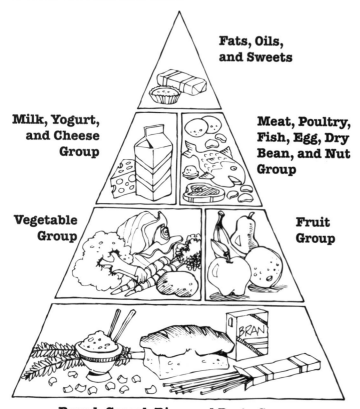

Fats, Oils, and Sweets

Milk, Yogurt, and Cheese Group

Meat, Poultry, Fish, Egg, Dry Bean, and Nut Group

Vegetable Group

Fruit Group

Bread, Cereal, Rice, and Pasta Group

WEATHER VANE

Directions: Color and cut out the pieces. Attach the pieces to a straw with staples. Connect the straw to a stick or a pencil with a pin. Put the stick in the ground in a windy place and observe the direction of the wind.

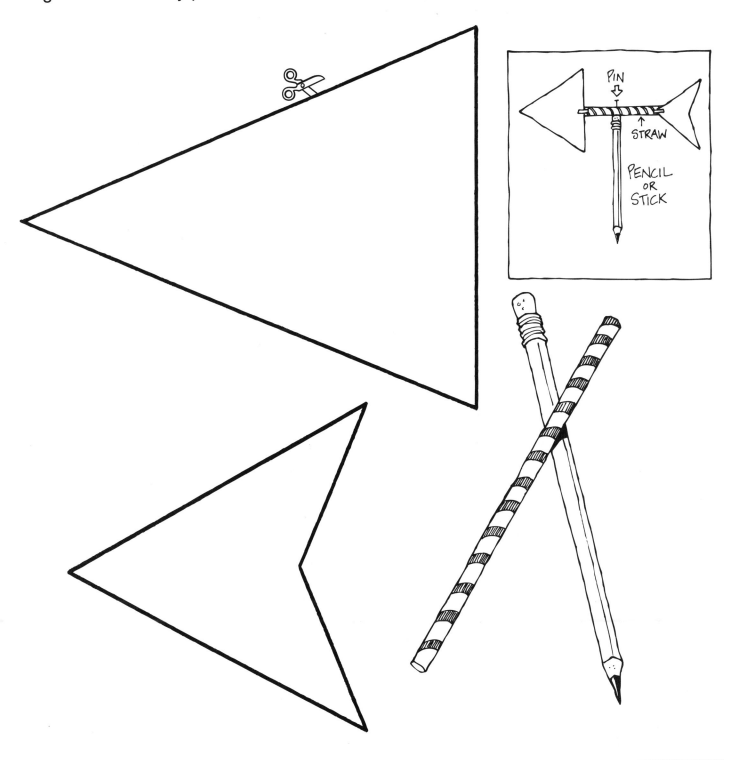

WINDMILL

Directions: Color and cut out the pieces. Overlap the flaps (see diagram 1). Push the pin through the flaps where indicated by the hole circle, through the center hole marked with a star, and through a short section of straw into a pencil eraser (diagram 2). Blow on the windmill to try it!

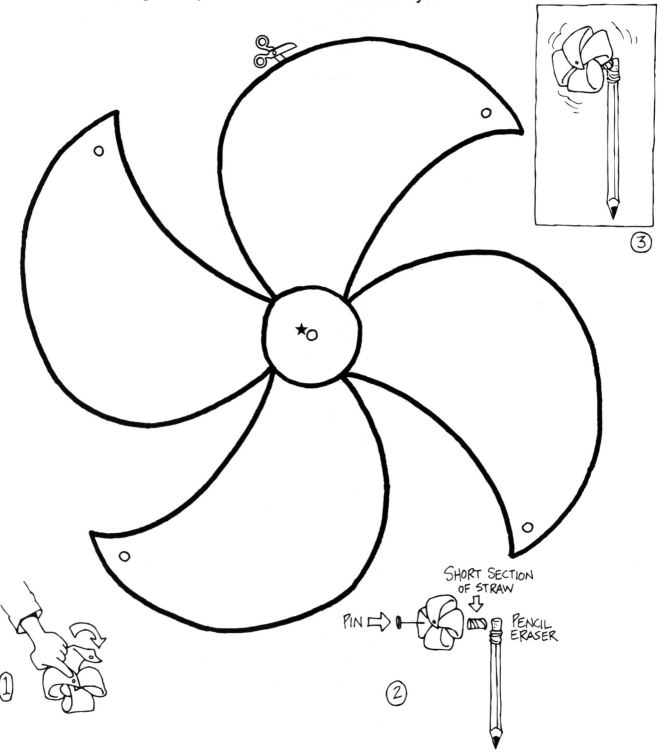

FS122003 Getting Ready to Teach First Grade

BUTTERFLY PATTERN

Directions: Color a symmetrical design on your butterfly. Cut the butterfly out along the dotted line.

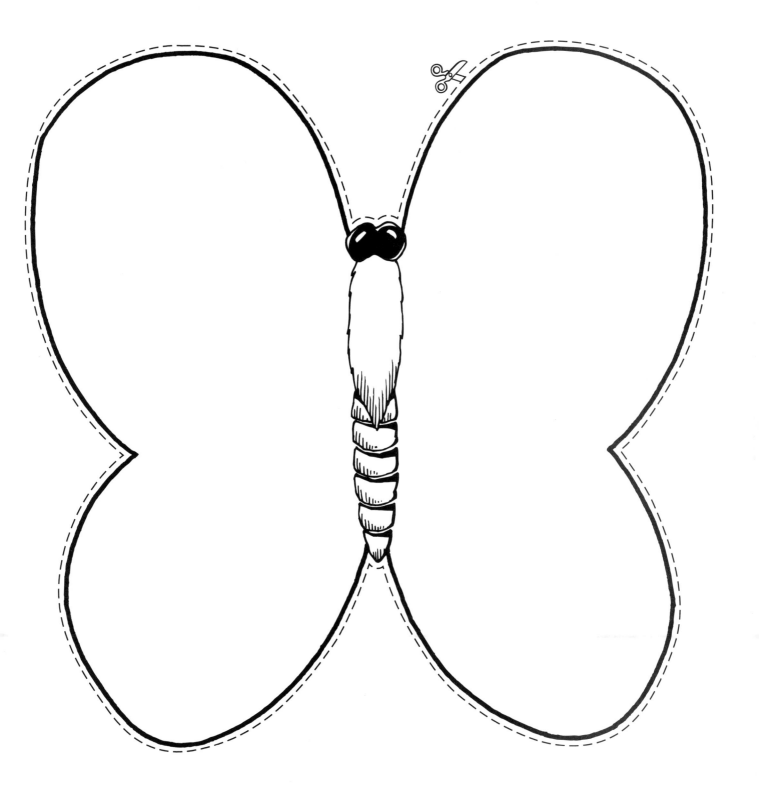

SOCIAL STUDIES

Skills

As with science and health, social studies subjects are commonly taught using thematic units. Following are examples of activities for thematic units designed to teach the social studies skills listed below.

- Listen to directions and to understand ideas.

- Locate and use information from pictures, books, and the five senses.

- Classify objects and pictures.

- Sequence a variety of things and ideas such as pictures, days of the week, months, personal experiences, and details of stories.

- Use indefinite time concepts such as *long ago* and *after* in discussions and in oral work.

- Dictate signs, captions, labels, and individual group stories.

- Answer questions with complete sentences.

- Identify the globe as a model of the earth.

- Identify, describe, construct, and read maps of the classroom, school, and neighborhood.

- Relate up and down, left and right, to the four cardinal directions on a map.

- Learn one's address and safest route to and from school.

- Use maps and globes when applying geographic skills.

- Identify, describe, and use symbols, titles, and legends on maps.

- Compare information and ideas from several different sources by interpreting pictures, relate words to pictorial content, and relate pictorial content to the main idea and details.

- Submit information for class charts, tables, and graphs. Read, identify, and explain information found on various charts, tables, and graphs.

> To regard teachers—in our entire educational system, from the primary grades to the university—as priests of our democracy is therefore not to indulge in hyperbole. It is the special task of teachers to foster those habits of open-mindedness and critical inquiry which alone make for responsible citizens, who, in turn, make possible an enlightened and effective public opinion.
>
> —Felix Frankfurter, opinion, <u>Wieman v. Updegraff</u>, 1952

- Apply information to new situations.

- Understand that problems keep occurring in life.

- Formulate and evaluate possible solutions to a problem.

- Clarify personal and family values.

- Identify pleasant and unpleasant feelings.

- Identify values conflict when related to the environment.

- Cooperate in planning projects and following through on group tasks.

- Recognize that all individuals live within a framework of law and order.

Social Studies Units

Example 1: Family

Art

Have each student trace one of his or her hands with a marker on thick white construction paper and cut it out. Then have the student write *My Family* on the palm of the hand. On each finger, have him or her draw a picture of a family member. Have the student draw a self-portrait on the thumb. Display the hands on a bulletin board in the room after students share their hands and introduce their family members to the class.

Math

After students introduce their family members to the class using the hand puppets, make a class graph representing family members in the class. Use butcher paper to set up the graph. Label the bottom portion of the graph with numbers 2 to 10. A student who has four family members would put his or her name in the "4" column. When the students finish putting their names on the graph, you can talk about it and ask questions. *Who has the most family members? Who has the least amount of people in their family? How many more four-member families are there than seven-member families?*

Research/Art

Making a family coat of arms gives students an opportunity to discover and take pride in their family heritages. Give each student a large piece of white construction paper. Show students how to draw the shape of a coat of arms—or provide them with copies of a coat-of-arms outline. Have the students divide the coat of arms into four sections. These sections honor the family's traditions, heritage, occupations, and members. Students can write or draw about these topics within the appropriate sections. They might even make a list of words that describe their families. This is a good lesson for teaching adjectives. When the students have written about their families, they can decorate their shields with paint, crayons, or markers.

Research/Art

Making a family tree is a great way for students to learn about their family history. As a homework assignment, it allows students and their parents to work together to place their ancestors on a family tree. They can be creative and use any materials they have available. When the students bring the trees back to class, they can share what they learned with their peers.

Writing

Encourage students to write about their families in their writing journals. Let them choose what they want to write about—a vacation they took, what they do together on the weekends, what their parents or siblings do, and so on. Have them invent family adventures using their imaginations.

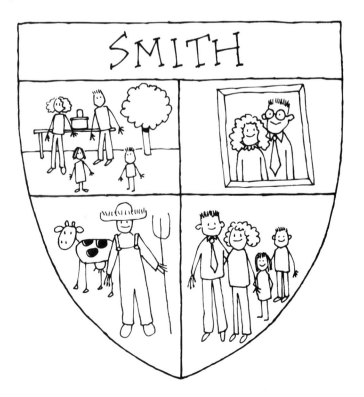

Example 2: Farms

Reading

Create a poetry chart using butcher paper and the poem below. Hang the chart on the wall in front of the students. Have the students listen as you read the poem to them. Then choral read or sing the poem all together. Brainstorm a list of picture clues that would help them to read the poem on their own. Finally, allow the students to create picture clues for the poem and paste them on the butcher paper around the words.

TO THE FARM
Sung to: "Twinkle, Twinkle, Little Star"

Donkeys, kittens, cows that moo,
Puppies, horses, chickens, too.
Fish that swim down in the pond.
Piglets oinking all day long.
All these animals you can see
If you go to the farm with me.

During this unit, the students can make farm poetry books. Give them copies of the poems you use. Have them make picture clues in their own books and practice reading the poems to their peers. Here are some other farm poems:

FARM SOUNDS
Sung to: "The Wheels on the Bus"

The cow in the barn goes moo, moo, moo.
Moo, moo, moo. Moo, moo, moo.
The cow in the barn goes moo, moo, moo.
All around the farm.

The duck in the pond goes quack, quack, quack.
Quack, quack, quack. Quack, quack, quack.
The duck in the pond goes quack, quack, quack.
All around the farm.

(Make up other verses that will go with this pattern.)

TAKE ME OUT TO THE BARNYARD
Sung to: "Take Me Out to the Ball Game"

Take me out to the barnyard.
Take me out there right now.
Show me the cows, pigs, and horses, too.
I hear an oink and a neigh and a moo.
There are chickens laying their eggs.
If they don't lay, it's a shame.
Oh, it's one, two, three eggs today,
And I'm glad I came.

Writing

Allow students to use their imagination by pretending they are farm animals. Have each student write a story from an animal's point of view. What is its life like? Who are its friends? What does it eat every day? Where does it sleep?

Art

Give students an opportunity to create the animals they wrote about in their stories. Have them brainstorm what materials—from among those available in the classroom—they could use to create texture on the animals. For example: for a pig, they could use pink cotton balls; for a goat, they could use sandpaper, and for a cow, they could glue on coffee beans. It might be helpful to reproduce animal patterns for the students to cut out first.

Science

Where does milk come from? If possible, take your students on a field trip to a dairy farm or show a video explaining this process. Next, give each student a copy of the sentence strips on page 62. Have the students cut out the strips and arrange them in order. Then have them glue the strips on paper and draw pictures to illustrate each step. This activity also reinforces students' sequencing skills.

Math

Distribute copies of the *Farm Math* worksheet on page 63. Allow pairs of students to work together to solve the problems. When finished, allow students to compare their answers with those of another group.

Other Social Studies Lessons

Jobs and Work

Invite parents as class guests to teach your students about their careers. You could also plan a field trip to visit a parent's place of employment. Designate a day for the students to come to school dressed in an outfit to represent one of their parents' jobs or the jobs the students would like to have some day.

Maps

Introduce maps to students. Explain what maps are used for and how to use them. Make a sample map of your school's neighborhood to use as an example. Then allow the students to create maps of their own neighborhoods, including where they live and the locations of schools, parks, libraries, stores, and other places of interest. This could be a homework assignment to be completed at home with parents.

Needs and Wants

Ask the students to talk about things they really want. If they could pick a few things they really want, what would they be? Then ask the students to tell you things they need in order to survive. Help the students identify what their needs are. While the students are brainstorming, make a list of their ideas on a T-chart on the chalkboard or on butcher paper. In preparation for this activity, collect pictures out of magazines that depict needs or wants. Hold up the pictures one at a time and let the students tell you if it is a need or a want. Have students write *I want…, I need…* sentences and draw pictures below them. Share the sentences and pictures with the class.

Directions: Cut out the strips below. Glue them on construction paper in the correct order. Draw a picture next to each sentence.

They are milked by machines.

The milk is delivered to stores.

The processing plant puts the milk into cartons.

Cows eat grass and hay.

Shoppers buy the milk.

The milk is pumped into big trucks.

Farm Math

Directions: Read each problem carefully. Draw a picture of the problem. Write the equation and solve it.

Read	Draw	Write
There are five cows eating grass. One cow lies down. How many cows are left eating grass?		
Three ducks are swimming in the pond. Two ducks jump in. How many ducks are swimming in the pond?		
One dog barks at a mouse. Another dog barks, too. How many dogs are barking?		
Seven horses run in the field. Two get tired and walk. How many horses are left running in the field?		
Two cats are stuck in a tree. The farmer rescues one cat. How many cats are left in the tree?		
Four pigs lie in the mud. Two get hungry and leave to eat. How many pigs are left lying in the mud?		
Six chickens are eating seed. One goes to sleep. How many chickens are left eating seed?		
Two farmers are plowing the fields. Nine farmers come to help. How many farmers are plowing the fields now?		

TECHNOLOGY

Technology requirements are changing daily. A general overview of the skills in this area is listed here for reference.

Skills

Industrial technology

- Identify shapes, sizes, and quantities of materials.

- Follow simple rules to construct projects.

- Learn to identify basic hand tools such as hammer, saw, tri-square, C-clamp, and safety block.

- Use tools safely and properly.

- Develop an awareness of assembly techniques, and the relationship between raw materials and finished products.

Computer technology

- Handle the hardware in appropriate ways.

- Develop familiarity with the computer keyboard.

- Use basic software tools and processes appropriately.

- Become familiar with drawing, painting, and word-processing software.

Industrial Technology

Students learn much about industrial technology through thematic units and exposure to related topics in literature. Whenever possible, compare the formal setting and rules of the classroom to the importance of safety and social order in our communities and government.

Industrial Technology Center Idea

Set up a career center with different occupational items. Include apparel representing different jobs, and let students dress up and pretend to work in those careers. Other items might include paper, envelopes, a mailbox, and stamps for postal workers; a first-aid kit with bandages, a toy doctor's kit, gowns, and slippers for medical careers; and a microscope, a calculator, a typewriter, and a ruler for careers in science, business, writing, and drafting.

Transportation Unit

When you teach on transportation, students learn about different modes of transportation and their respective functions. They should learn to recognize and classify vehicles according to the basic categories of air, land, and sea. Activities in a transportation unit might include visits to airports, bus depots, and train stations. Follow up field trips with related literature and writing projects. Students could, for example, write a story about a trip they took and what kinds of transportation they used. You can teach students about the progress of transportation over time, with comparisons between past and present transportation vehicles. Hands-on activities may include the construction of model vehicles and transportation systems.

One of my favorite transportation lessons is the "Imaginary Island." Divide the class into cooperative groups of three or four students. Give each group a large sheet of posterboard with a randomly shaped island drawn on it. Then have the students draw in airports, seaports, roads, train stations, railroad tracks, subway stations, and bus depots. They can also draw in houses, trees, beaches, stadiums, or whatever else their imaginations can come up with. After students finish creating and naming their islands, they present the final product to the class. You might also ask them to work together or individually to write a story about an imaginary trip to, from, or across the island.

> **Change is an ongoing process that takes time and courage. It is not easy to go beyond comfort and security to try new things . . . Savor the freedom of change.**
>
> —Miriam A. Leiva, National Council of Teachers of Mathematics

Computer Technology

Some schools will provide a computer lab, in which case you may not be directly responsible for creating and evaluating computer-related lessons or projects. If your school provides a computer lab teacher, work with him or her to coordinate projects and tasks with lessons in your classroom.

Many schools today provide one or more computers in the classroom. If your room includes a computer, take advantage of the many ways it can enrich the learning environment.

Educational software is readily available for virtually any subject imaginable. These interactive programs are not only educational, but quite entertaining as well. You'll be amazed at the level of concentration your students exhibit while engaged in a good computer program!

If you're fortunate enough to have a computer, you might also have access to the Internet. Try creating a class web page to post Writer's Workshop projects and various other examples of student work. This will allow parents with Internet access at home or at work to view their child's projects and keep up-to-date with the changing classroom. Coordinate with teachers across the country to arrange for e-mail "pen-pals." With the Internet, you can teach about the geography of the country and the world while your students communicate with other students in those locations.

First-Grade Software Applications

Multiple-Subject Software

Jump Start 1st Grade by Knowledge Adventure

Reader Rabbit's 1st Grade by The Learning Company

Fisher-Price Ready for School 1st Grade by Davidson

Big Thinkers 1st Grade by Humongous Entertainment

Madeline Classroom Companion: 1st & 2nd Grade by Creative Wonders

Award Winning: K-3 Educational Software

A to Zap! by Sunburst Communications

Bumptz Science Carnival by Theatrix Interactive, Inc.

Snootz Math Trek by Theatrix Interactive, Inc.

Trudy's Time & Place House by Edmark Corporation

My Make Believe Castle by LCSI/Virtual Entertainment

Kid Pix Studio Deluxe by Broderbund

VISUAL AND PERFORMING ARTS

Visual Arts

Skills

- Name, recognize, and describe colors, lines, shapes, values, and textures in art and objects in the environment.

- Increase awareness of objects, scenes, and events observed in the environment.

- Recall observations.

- Observe that things look different under varying conditions.

- Express ideas and feelings about works of art and objects in nature.

- In the creation of personal artwork, demonstrate personal expressions, original concepts, and expressive qualities and moods.

- Use varied subject matter such as people, animals, plans, places, and events.

- Express the following on two-dimensional surfaces: overlapping of forms; variations in color, size, shape, and texture; and repetition of line, shape, and color.

- Use a variety of drawing techniques: continuous line or action drawing; decorative, imaginative, or realistic styles; and varied effects with the points and sides of crayons, pencils, and chalk.

- Use a variety of painting techniques: dry and wet brush; stippling; spatter painting; finger painting; color mixing; and crayon-resist washes.

- Model and construct three-dimensional forms demonstrating a growing awareness of relative proportion and emphasis using clay, bread dough, and other materials.

- Apply basic principles of relief printing, including additive (building up a design) and subtractive (carving out a design) methods.

- Use contrasting colors in personal artwork: light and dark; bright and dull; and warm and cool.

- Consider and use all the art space available in the format provided.

- Organize objects of varying shapes, sizes, and textures into a three-dimensional arrangement.

- Grow in the ability to work with craft processes such as weaving, stitchery, and papier-mâché.

- Create artwork based on images from the visual environment, memory, and from the imagination.

- Take good care of supplies.

- Begin to appreciate art from other cultures and other periods of history.

- Recognize the role museums have in our society.

- Begin to recognize the aesthetic qualities of line, color, shape, value, texture, balance, emphasis, contrast, repetition, rhythm, and unity in visual artwork.

> We have to regard it as our sacred responsibility to unfold and develop each individual's creative ability as dim as the spark may be and kindle it to whatever flame it may conceivably develop.
>
> —V. Lowenfeld, Basic Aspects of Creative Thinking, 1961

Art and Craft Activities

Art is a form of creativity that allows students to use their imagination. The goal is for students to create their own art, not to copy what the teacher or one of the classmates has made. The best way to allow students choice and opportunity for creativity is to provide them with various materials and tell them to make something with those materials. You will be amazed what your students can create. Give them stencils, paint, sponges, paintbrushes, yarn, doilies, tissue paper, markers, and paper. You will see your students come alive with creativity. Provide photos of fine art of subjects you are studying in thematic units, so that students see a variety of interpretations of the concrete world. As long as you give your students freedom in art, you can also do guided art and craft projects with them. This allows the students to see a variety of ways to do different things with art. Below are some activities you could teach your students throughout the school year.

Paper Plate Masks

Students can use paper plates to create a variety of different decorative masks. These masks, which might depict a lion, a pig, or some other popular animal, could be used in plays, for Halloween, or just for fun. Cut facial features out of construction paper. Provide students with materials to paint the masks. They can decorate the masks with construction-paper pieces, colored dots, buttons, and other items, and use pipe cleaners, pine needles, or toothpicks for whiskers. If students plan to use the masks as disguises, help them cut the eye holes and remind them not to wear the masks while walking near traffic.

Paper Bag Hats

Students can use large paper bags to make hats. Have each student roll the bag down from the opening in an outward direction and keep rolling the bag down to the end of the hat. This will form the band of the hat. Let students decorate the hats with paint, markers, crayons, doilies, and other items.

Pencil Flower

You will need white basket-type coffee filters, washable markers, pencils, a spray bottle, and rubber bands. Give each student three or four coffee filters. Have students make designs on the coffee filters with the washable markers and stack the filters flat on top of each other. Then show students how to fold the filters together and attach them to the eraser at the end of a pencil with a rubber band. Let students spray the filters with water and watch the colors blend together to create a beautiful flower. When they are dry—open them up to shape them into flowers.

Mosaic Animals

Provide students with copies of animal patterns or let them draw and cut out their own. Then have students cut small (half-inch) squares out of various colors of construction paper and glue them on the animal shapes using a variety of designs.

Sponge Painting

You will need washable paint, paper plates or trays leftover from microwaveable food, paper, and sponges. Cut the sponges into different shapes. Put the paint onto paper plates or into trays, one color per plate. Then have students press the sponges onto the paint and stamp them on the paper to create beautiful designs experimenting with repeating patterns and how different colors relate to each other. This is a project that could be messy, so it's a good idea to invite a parent or an upper-grade student to assist you in supervising the artists at work. Students will also enjoy cutting their own sponge shapes.

Tissue-Paper Projects

Cut one-inch squares out of colored tissue paper. Provide students with different shapes cut out of construction paper. The shapes could include pumpkins, flowers, houses, hearts, soccer balls, or trees. Show students how to decorate their shapes using the tissue paper. Place the eraser end of a pencil in the center of a tissue-paper square, and fold the tissue paper up to wrap around the end of the pencil. Place glue on the wrapped end of the eraser, and use the pencil to push the tissue paper onto the shaped paper. Remove the pencil and repeat with other tissue squares until the entire shape is covered.

Performing Arts

First-grade students learn performing arts through plays, puppet shows, dancing, singing, reader's theater, and musical instruments. This is often their first year of getting out in front of a crowd to perform. Create opportunities in the classroom, such as author's chair in Writer's Workshop, to help familiarize your students with being in front of crowds. Setting aside time during the week for class sharing is always a good idea. Whether students choose to share something they brought from home, a Reader's Workshop project, a book they wrote, an art project, or whatever, the point is to get them comfortable with public speaking. As with most things, practice makes perfect.

Be careful about pressuring students too quickly, but continue to encourage each of them in making progress. We want them to enjoy speaking in front of their peers.

Puppet Shows

Collecting puppets should be on every teachers' hobby list. Children love to play with puppets. Puppets create opportunities for students to be creative and use their imaginations. Just sit back and watch them perform full-length puppet shows from their favorite fairy tales. Depending on the puppets you have, you might need to help them adapt the characters a bit. Use a large piece of butcher paper for the backdrop. The students can create the setting on the butcher paper to fit with the story. They might need to rehearse the script several times before performing in front of groups. Ask other teachers to bring their students to your room for the puppet show.

Music

Skills

- Identify changes in melody, including high-low and up-down.

- Identify a familiar song by hearing the melody alone or by hearing its rhythm clapped or played.

- Identify the number of phrases within a song.

- Recognize an introduction and a coda.

- Recognize a countermelody, such as an ostinato.

- Recognize chord changes in a simple accompaniment on autoharp, resonator bells, or guitar.

- Know that changes of dynamics and tempo affect the character of the music.

- Identify the sounds of selected instruments of the orchestra and differences among adult (female and male) and child's singing voices.

- Match a pitch and imitate short melodies with accuracy.

- Sing short songs, keeping the pulse or beat steady.

- Compare a phrase in music with a sentence in language presenting a thought.

- Sing melodies in major and minor modes.

> **TIP!**
>
> Link art and music by showing artwork from a particular era while listening to music from that era.

- Select appropriate dynamics and produce expressive tone color when singing.

- Play patterns of melody from familiar songs.

- Play the home tone on bells at the end of a song.

- Play the rhythm of the melody of familiar songs on a variety of percussion instruments.

- Imitate short patterns of rhythm on many percussion instruments.

- Play slow and fast on a percussion instrument.

- Respond to music with simple axial (swaying and bending) and locomotor (walking and running) movements.

- Represent the pulse or beat and rhythm of the melody with small movements such as clapping or tapping.

- Create movements that describe the sounds of selected instruments.

- Recognize, read, and write short patterns of melody and rhythm in blank notation.

- Draw an arc on the board or a large sheet of paper to represent phrase length.

- Create and sing short melodies.

- Create and play short patterns of melody on the bells.

Each of us has our personal gifts as a teacher and areas of the curriculum where we feel very comfortable and areas where we feel less so. Share resources with another teacher to strengthen program areas where you don't feel confident. The first-grade teacher next door may love to teach music, and hate the "mess" of visual arts. Work out a schedule to help each other out by "swapping" teaching expertise.

If you have no one available to swap with, consult with the school's resource or media teacher and the children's librarian at the local public library.

> **The trouble with music appreciation in general is that people are taught to have too much respect for music; they should be taught to love it instead.**
>
> —Igor Stravinsky, <u>New York Times Magazine</u>, September 27, 1964

Listen to Music

Expose students to different varieties of music, from classical to contemporary, and accustom them to listen intently to music. Instruct them in musical elements that will increase their appreciation and understanding of the different styles and forms.

Sing Songs

Children love to sing! Why not encourage your students to sing on a regular basis? You will find enjoyment in this activity just as much as your students. Poetry and song books are useful tools to help you learn new songs. Make a goal to teach your students one new song a week!

69

Easy-to-Make Musical Instruments

Tambourine

Have each student decorate the bottoms of two paper plates. Staple the plates almost completely together along the outside rims of the plates, decorated sides out. Put a handful of beans inside the plates and finish stapling.

Rain Stick

Use a cardboard tube from a roll of paper towels. Close one end with tape and paper. Twist a small coat hanger so that it fits inside. Add a handful of rice or beans. Close the open end with tape and paper. Cover the entire paper towel roll with brown paper from a paper bag reinforcing the closures at the end. Decorate the rain stick to look like wood. You may find pliers or a wire cutter helpful for working with the hanger.

Papier-Mâché Maracas

Each student will need a cardboard tube from a roll of toilet paper and a balloon. Use the following directions to guide students in making their maracas. Inflate the balloon and tape it to the end of the tube so that it is secure. Using flour and water and small strips of newspaper, you will wrap papier-mâché strips around the roll and the balloon to create a maraca. Mix the flour and water to form a glue (1 cup flour; 1 cup water). Dip the newspaper into the glue and wipe off the extra liquid. Cover the maraca with overlapped newspaper, leaving a small hole at the top of the balloon. Let the maraca dry overnight. The next day, poke a hole in the balloon through the small hole at the top and fill the maraca with beans. Cover the hole with papier-mâché, and let it dry another night. When the maraca is completely dry, the students can paint their maracas with different colors and designs. Most types of paint will work. When the maracas have dried, they are ready to shake.

Drums

Each student can make a hand drum with a coffee or soup can, a rubber band, and a balloon. Use these directions to guide the students' efforts. Cut off the bottom portion of the balloon. Pull the balloon around the opening of the can so that it is secure. Put the rubber band around the balloon to hold it in place. Let students practice tapping on the drums to different rhythms and beats. When they are familiar with the beat, chant along with the drums.

> ### TIP!
>
> *Sing new information to your students. Sing instructions, sing number patterns, sing something your students have heard you say before. Even if your voice is not the world's best, your students will enjoy learning information this way. And your musically inclined students will learn more easily.*

CHAPTER THREE: THE CLASSROOM

ORGANIZATION

When you are preparing for the school year and setting up your class arrangement, developing order must be a top priority. A disorderly room has a tendency to make students disorderly too. Maximize space and provide for movement of the students. We don't want our students climbing over each other when they are lining up for recess. Make sure there is a place for each item in the classroom. This will help maintain your valuable teaching materials and books, so that you don't have to replace everything before the next year.

Depending on your philosophy of teaching, you may want to arrange your students into cooperative table groups. Label each group with a name that can be used as another teaching tool. Hang the name from the ceiling directly above the table group with a picture that represents the name. You could use the names of geometric shapes, such as *Spheres*, *Cones*, *Cylinders*, and *Cubes*, or the names of language arts terms, such as *Nouns*, *Verbs*, *Adjectives*, and *Pronouns*. These concepts are easily taught when the students interact with them daily.

TIP!

Reinforce left to right subtly in your room set up. Daily routines should be organized so that students are beginning activities posted at their left and moving to their right.

Sample Daily Schedule

Daily Schedule
School Day 8:00–2:30

8:00 Entry Task

8:15 Opening and Community Time

8:50 Math

9:30 Recess

9:45 Reader's Workshop Full Group Instruction/ Guided Reading/ Independent Work/ Centers

10:55 Spelling/Phonics

11:10 Lunch

11:55 Shared Oral Reading

12:20 M, W–Writer's Workshop
T, Th–Science/ Social Studies
F–Art

1:20 Recess

1:30 M, W, F–Physical Education
T, Th–Writing and Music

2:15 Closing

2:30 Dismissal

> The condition of the true artisan, perhaps, is most nearly akin to the gifted schoolteacher's: an all but anonymous calling that allows for mastery, even for a sort of genius, but rarely for fame, applause, or wealth, whose chief reward must be the mere superlative doing of the thing.
>
> —John Barth, <u>Teacher: The Making of a Good One</u>, Harper's, 1986

Scheduling

Following a daily schedule will make you more effective as a teacher. Schedules let the students know what is coming next and help keep you on track. To make a schedule, start by finding out what times may be planned for you already. Your school may have music, art, or science programs that regularly require students to be away from your classroom. There are usually scheduled recess or lunch times. You may have scheduled yard, bus, or lunchroom duties.

Divide the day into blocks of time for each subject. Opportunities to read, write, and work with mathematics should occur every day. Your school or district may have requirements about the minimal amount of time that should be devoted to certain subjects. Consider how to maximize your teaching assistant's time.

Keep in mind as you develop a class schedule that your first graders will probably be more focused in the morning than in the afternoon. School is stimulating, and your students will get tired.

Entry Task

No matter how hard we try, there tends to be disorder each morning when the students arrive. You are constantly being handed notes from parents, field trip slips, lunch money, you name it. Students invariably have something they want to tell you or share with you. It is probably the most important time of the day, because it will set the tone for the rest of the day. So how do you handle this commotion?

At the beginning of the year, set up as part of the daily routine an activity for the students to do when they walk into the classroom. I call it an entry task. When the students enter the classroom and put their coats, bags, and lunches away, there is a task written on the chalkboard for them to do. It may be journal writing, silent reading, solving a math problem, or sitting on the carpet ready to listen. Train your students to look for their task each morning.

Many first-grade students begin the year unable to read. Compensate for this by setting up a schedule of entry tasks. Maybe you want them to spend the first 10 minutes of class with a book. If you do this every day, you eventually won't need to write it on the board. This approach will give you time in the morning to greet your students, conference, organize lunch money, and handle any surprises. Start the day off right!

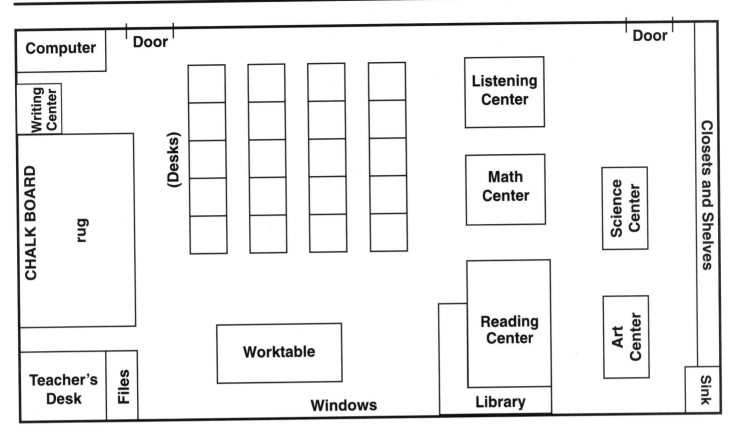

Centers

Incorporating centers into your daily schedule provides students with an opportunity to interact socially and cooperatively with their peers while engaging in meaningful learning experiences. When planning your centers, you should consider the logistics of 25 first graders moving around the room and determine which kinds of centers you will have. It is unlikely that you will have sufficient room for all of the possible centers to occur at the same time.

Reading Center

Every class should have a reading center. Include some of the following items in this center to make it comfortable for readers: beanbag chairs, a mini-tent, body-length pillows, a futon mattress, a small couch, cushioned foldout chairs, and sleeping bags. If possible, place your reading center in a quiet corner of the room, secluded from noisy areas or centers, to ensure uninterrupted reading time.

If you don't have a bookshelf available, there are other resources you can use to store your books in.

Students choose books based upon their interests, so they should be able to see the front covers of the books. They have a hard time choosing books placed on a bookshelf with only the spines showing. Dishwashing bins or plastic baskets work well, because they allow students easy access to flip through the books. Place the bins on a table nearby or on the floor in the reading center. I like to have several bins placed all around the room for other reading times provided in class.

Math Center

This is a center where children can explore and be creative with all the manipulatives they use throughout the year. You might include the following items: play money, pattern blocks and cards, counters of various types, flash cards, geo-boards and rubber bands, place value blocks and mats, a magnetic money tray, and a variety of math games, dice, flashcards, and linking cubes.

Art Center

Since art is all about creativity, the art center should maximize a child's ability to be creative. There are numerous materials you can provide for students in an art center. Rotating these materials throughout the year will encourage the students to try new things. Materials you may consider providing are stencils, markers, crayons, colored pencils, stamps, different types of paints, tissue paper, yarn, beads, a variety of colored construction paper, different shapes of paper, drawing paper, paintbrushes, sponges, hole punches, scissors, glue, glitter, wax paper, string, buttons, ink pads, how-to-draw books, and paper towel roll tubes. The list goes on and on. When provided with several materials, students will often use them in creative and unexpected combinations. You may also want to put examples of craft ideas in the art center. While students enjoy making their own things, they also appreciate getting ideas and knowing how to make different crafts.

Listening Center

A listening center should include an audio player with headphones and cassettes with which students can listen to books on tape and other narrated stories. This center can provide motivation to read for some students. Try to allow as much freedom as possible in this center, and offer a variety of books and stories. Because this is a quiet place, it is a good center to locate next to the reading center.

Story-Telling Center

This center encourages creativity and dramatic play. The items useful in this center include a variety of hand puppets, a flannel board, flannel board pieces, and a small stage. Have students use the puppets and flannel boards to make up scripts and stories of their own. Give them opportunities to perform these stories for their classmates. You can add more structure to this center by providing scripts for students. Even if some students aren't quite ready to read the scripts, they will be encouraged and motivated to learn by their presence.

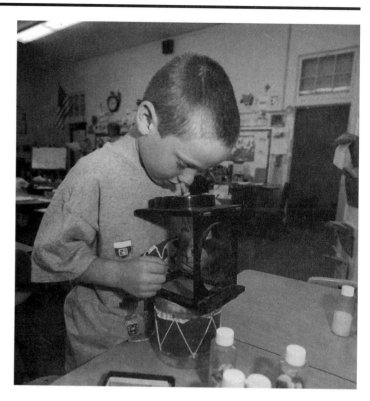

Computer Center

If you have a computer, try to create space for more than one student to sit at the computer at a time. Locate your computer away from heating objects, dusty areas, and water sources.

Science Center

Vary this center according to thematic units and lessons being addressed in the classroom. Stock the center with the materials necessary for various extension activities. For example, if you are teaching a science unit on magnets, this center should include magnets, objects that are attracted to magnets, objects that are not attracted to magnets, books about magnets, and games to play with magnets. Try to keep a collection of books near this center that contain science center activities. Students enjoy looking at the pictures and trying to duplicate different experiments.

Language Center

This center should focus on creative writing. Materials useful in this center include magazines, alphabet stamps, picture stamps, stamp pads, writing paper, pencils, colored pencils, erasers, and stencils. Encourage students to use the stamps and pictures to create their own stories.

Building Center

Block building is developmentally appropriate for students through grade three. The process lets children practice eye-hand coordination and use their creativity. Standard blocks work well in this center, as do little plastic animals, interlocking blocks, building logs, and other assembly items found in toy stores. This center tends to be one of the noisier parts of the classroom.

Puzzles and Games Center

Puzzles and games are an excellent way to encourage cooperative learning. Numerous games are on the market that promote learning for all levels. You can rotate games and puzzles throughout the year to create variety. Allow a space in your class where the students can spread out on the floor to tackle games and puzzles. Often you can store the games and puzzles on a shelf and tell the students where to take them.

Wall Charts

Wall charts are helpful teaching and learning tools in the classroom. Providing a print-rich environment allows students yet more opportunities to read. You will find your students reading these charts during independent work time. Here are some wall charts you can make that will foster literacy. Personalize each chart by a teacher/student brainstorm session.

Describing words

smart, pretty, beautiful, ugly, prickly, shiny, sparkly, smooth, graceful, colorful, red, blue, green, yellow, bright, round, delicious, sweet, solid, soft, hard, crisp, oval, square, crunchy, golden, rotten, happy, sad, rough, stinky, ragged, bumpy, glorious, spectacular, radiant

Beginning Story Phrases

Once upon a time…   Years and years ago…

Once there was…   First…

In the beginning…   It all started when…

One day…   One dark night…

> The classroom and teacher occupy the most important part, the most important position of the human fabric . . . In the schoolhouse we have the heart of the whole society.
>
> —Harry Golden, So Long as You're Healthy: Teacher's Revolution, 1970

Yesterday…   One morning…

Today…   One lovely…

Once there lived…   One rainy…

It was one of those days…   One beautiful…

A long time ago…   In the middle of the..

Let me begin my story…   Have you ever…?

Last year…   Let me tell you…

When I was little…

Middle Story Phrases

Then…   The next day…

After awhile…   When…

In the middle…   Second…

Suddenly…   Who…

After that…   Let's get on with the story…

The story goes on…   Months later…

Days later…

Ending Story Phrases

Finally…   and that's the end of my story.

In the end…   That was it.

At last…   The end.

…happily ever after.   …friends to the end.

They were friends forever.   …had fun.

They had a happy life.   Goodbye.

The problem was solved.

The Editing Process

Did I use capital letters correctly?
Did I use punctuation marks?
Did I spell each word correctly?
Does it make sense?
Is my handwriting neat and readable?

The Writing Process

(This is a part of the Writer's Workshop program.)

1. Write a story, a letter, or a poem.

2. Edit your work.

3. Conference with your teacher.

4. Publish (make a book).

5. Illustrate your book.

6. Read your book to three people.

7. Go to the author's chair.

8. Go back to number 1 and write!

Topics to Write About

(Personalize this list by brainstorming additions to it with your students.)

vacations
one person you would want to meet and why
book characters
school
holidays
magic
your family
cars
if you had three wishes
animals
hobbies
movies
favorite foods
babies
songs
letters
changes
flying
recipes
happy times in your life
ocean
how to do something
nonfiction and fiction stories
rainbows
retell an event
true facts
giants
recess
persuade someone to do something
compliments
your pet
your teacher
problems and solutions
if you had 100 dollars
your babysitter
something you learned
a place you would like to visit and why
the future
yourself
people you love
what you want to be when you grow up
places you have visited
scary things
something funny or sad

Cooperative Learning

Cooperative learning fosters social skills along with academic skills and prepares students to function successfully in their communities. When students work together, they learn the value of teamwork and problem solving. Encourage cooperative learning by setting up your students' desks in groups. Arrange students so that different ability levels are represented in each group.

Giving Students "Helper Jobs"

Giving students responsibilities in the classroom helps them feel like important, contributing members of the community. Our goal is to create a community environment in which everyone accepts responsibility for contributing to the classroom's overall good. Make a list of classroom jobs on a sheet of chart paper. Next to each job, attach a clothespin with a student's name on it. These are the student helpers for the week. Rotate the clothespins weekly and try to allow every student to perform every job. Jobs may include teacher helpers, calendar, attendance, flag salute leader, line leader, floor monitor, lunch basket, pencil sharpener, chalkboard cleaner, and pencil sharpener cleaner.

RECORD KEEPING AND ASSESSMENT

Reading Record Files

Reading Record files were discussed previously on page 20. They are mentioned here as a reminder of the role they play in the overall organization of the classroom. These files are also useful when conducting parent-teacher conferences. All of your information is located in one place, and you can refer to it when explaining students' strengths and areas needing improvement.

Writing Record Files

You may also want to create a Writing Record File for each student. Individual conferencing with students occurs often in the Writer's Workshop program. This file will provide an excellent way to keep notes of each student's writing progress.

Write your students' names on the files and store them in a convenient place near where you conduct your individualized student conferences. Each time you conference with a student, write down what the student wrote (a story, a letter, etc.), what the student needs work on, and what the student's strengths are. Using these files, you will notice how much progress each student makes throughout the year.

A Winner...

Makes time.

Says, "I'll plan to do that."

Says, "Let's find out."

Says, "I'm good, but not as good as I can be."

Empowers.

Listens.

Says, "If it is to be, it is up to me."

Catches people doing things right.

Is not afraid of losing.

Says, "I was wrong."

Wants to.

Sees opportunities.

Is part of the solution.

Celebrates others.

Does it!

Expects success.

Makes commitments.

Works harder.

Portfolios

Reading and writing files consist of recorded observations made by you or your assistant. Portfolios, on the other hand, are collections of student work created throughout the year. Create a portfolio folder for each student and store it in an easily accessible location. As the school year advances, choose representative works from each student to include in his or her portfolio. Generally speaking, the more samples collected, the better. However, stuffing portfolios with each and every completed task will not guarantee a quality result. Choose samples that demonstrate target skills, progress, or areas needing improvement. Reader's Workshop final projects and "published" projects should almost always be included. Date each entry and file them in chronological order. This will allow you to flip through the pages and view the student's progress. You may also make notes on pages to remind you why a particular entry was included.

Portfolios become a valuable resource during parent meetings. When portfolios are presented in combination with reading and writing files, parents will appreciate not only their child's progress, but your professionalism as well. In some instances, recorded observations in reading and writing files will correspond with entries in the student's portfolio. Toward the end of the school year, perhaps at an open house, these portfolios can be given to parents, if they are not to become part of the school's permanent records. Advise parents of the benefits of keeping the portfolio for later reference. Second-grade teachers might find the information helpful in establishing the student's current skill level and needs.

Speaking and Listening Checklists

Use the form on page 79 when you have an opportunity to observe students interacting in the classroom, or whenever you observe a notable speaking or listening behavior. Parents will surely be interested in these kinds of observations.

Grade Book

A grade book will help you track scores on tests, homework projects, and miscellaneous academic skills. Review the report card you must complete for each student before you set up your grade book so that you can organize yourself to track the specific information you need to report.

Depending on the school where you teach, a grade book may or may not be a critical tool. Some schools will require a strict record of scores for computing final grades, while others will measure progress and be less concerned about each and every score. An accurate grade book is useful to document your assessment process.

Speaking Checklist

	Observations	Frequent	Occasional	Rare	Comments
Vocabulary	Limited				
	Expanded				
Group Interaction	Participates in Conversation				
	Participates in Discussion				
Uses Language for	Describing				
	Exploring				
	Reasoning				
	Questioning				
	Narrating				
Syntax	Simple				
	Complex				

Listening Checklist

	Observations	Frequent	Occasional	Rare	Comments
Understanding a message	Recalls details				
	Recalls sequence				
	Follows directions				
	Identifies main idea				
Analyzing a message	Identifies fact and opinion				
	Forms opinions				
Responding to a message	Listens for enjoyment				
	Appreciates the sound of language				
	Listens and responds to others				
	Identifies point of view and feelings				

CHAPTER FOUR: RELATIONSHIPS

CLASSROOM MANAGEMENT

First-grade students are full of energy and enthusiasm. The challenge we face is to channel this energy and enthusiasm into learning. An effective classroom management policy will help students stay on task and allow us to teach, instead of simply monitoring the behavior of students for six or more hours a day! More than a list of rules and consequences, a classroom management system establishes an environment of mutual respect and creative freedom.

Class Rules

To maintain a positive and safe classroom environment, classroom rules should be established during the first day of class. Students will know what expectations you have of them and what they can and cannot do in the classroom. The big question is which rules to use. If you keep the number of rules to a minimum, the students can more easily remember them. Rules should be broadly stated and should cover a wide variety of unacceptable behaviors. Give your students ownership in determining the rules, and you will be on your way toward a community atmosphere.

> **As you look at your youngsters, be sure that your standards of promptness, of attention, of quiet, of courtesy, are realistically geared to children, not idealistically geared to angels.**
>
> —James L. Hymes, Jr., <u>The Oldest Order Changeth</u>, NEA Journal, April 1953

On the first day of school, have a list of three to five rules in mind you want the students to follow throughout the year. When you sit the students down to discuss rules, allow them to explain what they think the rules should be. The great part is that—most likely—you will guide the students to the rules you have already in your mind. Popular rules used in first-grade classrooms include the following:

Do your best.
Use an inside voice.
Keep your hands, feet, and objects to yourself.
Respect others.
Follow directions.
Raise your hand.
Work and play safely.

Quiet Signals

At the beginning of the school year, establish a quiet signal to use when requesting the students' attention. There are several different options and you will need to decide which one works best for you. I have found that counting slowly down from five is very effective because it gives the students time to finish a sentence, put their pencils down, or mark their place. Other signals include "Give me five," "May I have your attention please?" "Freeze," counting up to 10, clapping in a rhythm and the students repeating you, and ringing a bell. When you say "Give me five," you put your hand up showing five fingers and the students drop what they are doing and put their hands up, too. Whatever signal you choose, make sure you remain consistent, and wait to speak until everyone is ready to listen.

Pull-Card Chart

Establishing consequences for misbehavior is a vital part of your classroom management system. Students need to know that certain results will follow when your expectations are not met, and rules are broken. A card chart is an effective way to set up this system.

Take a large piece of posterboard and glue library pockets on it. Make a pocket for each student in your class. Laminate the posterboard and cut slits with a razor blade where the pockets open. You will place four index cards inside of the pockets as follows: in front, a card with a green dot; then one with a yellow dot; then a red dot; and finally, at the back, one with a black dot. Students begin the day with a green dot showing. If they misbehave, you instruct them to pull a card. They will then be on a yellow dot, which is a warning. If they pull another card and are then on the red dot, they will miss a recess. If they pull the last card and are then on a black dot, you will need to call home or send them to the principal. You can decide what the consequences are, but make sure you enforce them. Post the consequences next to the chart so the students are reminded of them daily. Motivate your students with a sign that shows what each dot symbolizes: (Green dot) = Go for the green! You are doing great! (Yellow dot) = Remember the rules. (Red dot) = Stop and think.

Grouping Students

Begin the year by putting colored dots for labeling on each student's name tag. Use the colors yellow, green, black, red, and blue. Divide the different colored dots among the students. For example, if you have 20 students, there will be five students per color. Create a chart to hang on the wall that lists the days of the week and the dots that correlate with the day. For example:

Monday—(yellow dot)

Tuesday—(green dot)

Wednesday—(black dot)

Thursday—(blue dot)

Friday—(red dot)

Place the sticker next to the day (you don't need to write the words "yellow dot"). Use this system for many routines in your class. Monday is the yellow dot day, so on Monday the yellow dot group will line up first, share, choose centers first, and so on. On Tuesday the green dot group takes over those jobs. This is an easy way to organize your classroom, and it provides the students with clear direction.

I've come to the frightening conclusion that I am the decisive element in the classroom. My personal approach creates the climate. My daily mood makes the weather. As a teacher, I possess a tremendous power to make a child's life miserable or joyous. I can be a tool of torture or an instrument of inspiration. I can humiliate, humor, hurt, or heal. In all situations, it is my response that decides whether a crisis will be escalated or de-escalated, a child humanized or dehumanized.

—Haim Ginott

SCHOOL STAFF

Entering a new teaching position in a new school can be overwhelming at first. You need to learn the curriculum and set up your classroom, and become acquainted with staff members and administrators. You wonder to whom you can turn for guidance and ideas. Other teachers are wonderful professional development resources. Use the *Staff Directory and Contact List* on page 90 to help you remember staff members' names and their positions in the school. Include room numbers and phone extensions, if applicable.

Colleagues

In many cases, the most valuable resources for teachers are found in the very buildings in which they teach. Never neglect the cumulative knowledge of your peers. Begin to establish relationships with your fellow teachers as soon as possible—perhaps even prior to the school year. Consider the benefits of a "team teaching" approach with other first-grade teachers, or simply get together regularly to brainstorm ideas and plan lessons. Combined classroom activities may provide you and other teachers with a more flexible schedule and create extra time for preparation. Teachers often send misbehaving students to other classrooms. Discuss these arrangements with other teachers to clarify expectations and avoid problems resulting from miscommunication.

In addition, building rapport with teachers throughout the building will create opportunities for you to gain ideas without directly seeking them. In one school, for example, teachers would meet at a local restaurant following school on Friday. They would celebrate the conclusion of yet another week while getting to know one another better. In the midst of a voluntary recreational get-together, lesson plans were discussed, classroom management procedures were refined, and ideas were swapped.

Teacher Assistants

Some schools provide teachers with classroom assistants. These individuals are usually designated to help with the students. If your assistant is there one hour a day, schedule your day accordingly to allow the assistant to work with the students one-on-one. Individualized reading conferences are always a good idea and a terrific way to use any help you have. If you are teaching a math lesson, have the assistant work with students individually on areas needing improvement.

Custodian

Get to know the custodian(s) of the school. They know where everything is. When you need furniture, special cleaning tools, light bulbs, and paper towels, talk to the custodian. They are powerful. Teach students to be responsible for cleaning the classroom at the end of each day. This will make the custodian's job a lot easier, and create an ally for you. There will come the day that your students have had a big party, you have all been painting, and several students drop paint water on the floor, and you will need special help cleaning.

Other Human Resources

Many schools have teachers who provide special services such as a reading laboratory, coordinate the art or music program, or manage the instructional materials owned by the school. They may be called resource teachers. Frequently resource teachers will be able to answer questions or make suggestions about educational and classroom management issues. In some schools where the principal is extremely busy, the resource teacher is the first person you ask for educational program support.

The school librarian can be another strong resource for you. Frequently school libraries have a regularly scheduled time when your students will go the library to learn about the resources there, enjoy literacy activities, read, and check out books. The school librarian knows what books are in the library and can help you find literature and non-fiction that will support your educational program.

The people who run the office keep the school moving. This is a tremendous job. Every piece of paper that comes to the school goes through the office. Attendance, payroll, mail, bulletins, field trip requests, book orders, and all official outbound papers are handled by the front office. Ask questions and get familiar with the procedures. Find out about deadlines for field trip requests, inter-district mail, and other information from the front office.

Many schools and districts have a school nurse full- or part-time. The nurse will coordinate hearing and vision screenings, keep medical information on students with health problems, and often has an office with beds where students who have taken ill can lie down. If you are concerned about a student's health, consult the nurse. He or she may also be able to help you find resources to assist the families of your students who need health care services.

HOME/SCHOOL CONNECTION

Back-to-School Night

Your goal on Back-to-School Night is to introduce yourself to the parents, let them know how excited you are to work with them, and explain what their child will be learning in your classroom. Create a packet of information to explain your philosophy of teaching without omitting any critical points that you might otherwise forget because of nervousness. Walk parents through this packet, pointing out certain information as you go. You may want to include a class list, the rules and consequences of the classroom, your homework policy, contact information, absence policy, a wish list for items you need, a list of reading strategies for the parents to use at home, a parent-student questionnaire, and a paragraph about yourself and your teaching philosophy. Parents will appreciate the effort you take in putting this together, and they will refer to it throughout the year.

Parent-Teacher Conferences

Parent-teacher conferences are an important part of your job. They can be rewarding experiences because you learn more about your students and you often hear how the parents feel about you as a teacher. You also get to show them samples of their children's work.

Have each student's portfolio available to show parents what their child has been doing. Parents are always thrilled to see the growth in their child as well as the projects he or she is working on.

Keep the conference positive. Always begin by focusing on the student's strengths. When discussing an area in which improvement is needed, use a positive tone and indicate how the child is working toward improvement.

> This is what knowledge really is. It is finding out something for oneself with pain, with joy, with exultancy, with labor, and with all the little ticking, breathing moments of our lives, until it is ours as that only is ours which is rooted in the structure of our lives.
>
> —Thomas Wolfe, <u>The Web and the Rock</u>, 1939

Encourage parents to work with their child at home by giving them ideas they can use to improve skills. Always end the conference with an encouraging comment, and let the parents know how much you enjoy working with their child.

Volunteers

Encourage parents to take part in their child's classroom. Let them know they are welcome to visit the classroom at any time. During Back-to-School Night, set out your Volunteer Sign-Up Sheet (page 91) and ask parents to sign it before they leave.

Volunteers come into your classroom to help, so make them feel comfortable. Allow them to choose what to do. Ideally, have them work with students. The more one-on-one help students get, the more progress they will make. Yet, not all volunteers are comfortable working with students, so be sure to offer other ways they can help. This takes organization on your part, but your time spent helping others help you is always worth it.

TIP!

Periodically send thank-you notes to your volunteers to let them know how appreciated they are.

CHAPTER FIVE: CLOSING THOUGHTS

ENGLISH LANGUAGE DEVELOPMENT

Students who speak a language other than English at home will need certain provisions to help them succeed at school. They may not speak or comprehend the English language, and even if they do, they will most likely experience difficulty.

The English language development program you use in your classroom will depend on the school or district you work in. Your district might have a formal plan for you to use when teaching ELD students.

Students with little-to-no English need time to orient themselves to the English language when they enter the classroom each day. They may seem to be unmotivated when in fact they are simply adjusting to the language. Be patient with them, and try to understand what a challenge they face in living with two different languages in two seemingly different worlds. What can we do to teach these students?

The Reader's Workshop and Writer's Workshop programs help these students tremendously because of their individualized approach. Throughout your lessons, use several visual items for students who lack English comprehension. Teaching with a thematic approach also helps. Giving students continual exposure to similar concepts will increase their level of comprehension. If you are teaching in a school with ELD students, ask other teachers and resource specialists for guidance. There are people designated to help out with these kinds of challenges.

MAINSTREAMING

Since first grade is the first year in a formal classroom setting, it is often the time when some students are identified with learning disabilities. Don't worry if you are not experienced with learning disabilities. You will know if a student is having difficulty because he or she will be noticeably behind most other students academically. If this should happen, contact your resource specialist, and have him or her observe the child and help you identify the learning disability. The resource specialist should help you decide which interventions will work best for a particular student with a learning problem.

There can be a temptation to label children with learning disabilities prematurely. Individual time with each student will enable you to catch the symptoms early and determine your next course of action. Keep records of observable behavior patterns and open communication with parents. Ask parents if they observe similar behaviors at home. Remember that all children have different learning styles, so you will need to balance developmentally appropriate activities with teaching strategies to engage each student. Below is a list of some common behaviors students will display that might indicate a learning problem.

- Unable to work on something for longer than 30 seconds

- Unable to hear you

- Unable to hold a pencil or form a letter

- Continuously acts out

- Difficulty recognizing sight words or words they have been continually exposed to

- Unable to see the chalkboard

- Difficulty engaging in lessons

- Difficulty paying attention

- Unable to sit still for longer than five minutes

- Laughing at inappropriate times

COMMUNITY RESOURCES

The community resources you use for instruction will depend largely on the area in which you are located. However, there are common places found in most cities you can visit on field trips. Always remember to contact the place you wish to visit to ask if they provide guided tours for visiting classrooms. You might be surprised at some of the places that provide instructional tours of their facilities and functions.

Another way to use community resources is to invite guest speakers to the classroom. For example, you may want to invite a Native American to teach your students about his or her people's history and culture. Or you may want to invite a police officer to teach about safety. You have a variety of options.

Places to Consider for Field Trips

Zoo

Planetarium

Fire Department

Greenhouse

Museums

Airport

Hospital

Bus Terminal

Library

Fish Hatchery

Indian Reservation

Pumpkin Patch

Farms

Train Station

Parks

Police Station

Grocery Stores

Farmers' Market

Restaurants

Nursery

County Fair

Dairy Farm

MATERIALS CHECKLIST

Materials to Acquire

student name tags for desks

stacking trays

children's books

pocket charts

grade book

book display case

lesson plan book

white erase board

manila file folders

electric pencil sharpener

hanging files

three-hole punch

round stickers of various colors for labeling

two-hole punch

dictionary

stamps

bulletin board borders and decorations

ink pads

labels

stickers

mailboxes (cubbies) for each student

library pockets

plastic storage bins

Velcro® and magnetic strips

stapler

scissors

tape dispenser

Items Parents Might Donate

books

carpet squares

facial tissue

pencils

bookmarks

stickers

stamps

stencils

puppets

games

puzzles

plastic storage bins

erasers

markers

sponges

liquid hand soap

art materials

paintbrushes

paint shirts

copy paper

fans

children's videos

computer programs

house plants

items for the classroom store

WHEN YOU ARE ABSENT

Even if you enjoyed perfect health before you started working as a teacher, you will get sick. You are exposed to lots of germs in a school. Usually by your third year of teaching your immunity is built enough so that you don't catch every cold or other virus that walks through your classroom door. In addition, in-service conferences may be scheduled during the school day so that you must be away from your classroom.

Your school or district may have a service that arranges for substitutes or you may have to find your own. At the beginning of the year, find out what you need to do by asking another teacher or the school secretary. If you are able, leave plans for the substitute teacher. Use the form on page 92 to communicate with your "sub."

CHILD ABUSE

In many states teachers are required by law to report any suspicion of child abuse. Proving abuse is not your responsibility, but reporting suspicions of abuse is. Some schools will follow up a teacher's suspicions, other schools require the teacher to act alone. Check with your school or district about your legal responsibilities.

REPORT CARD COMMENTS

When it comes time to fill out report cards, you usually have the option of providing comments. With 20 or more student report cards to complete, you might start feeling like you're saying the same things about very different students. Here's a list of comments to help you along.

Working at grade level

Uses time wisely

Easily distracted

Enjoys working independently

A pleasure to have in class

Always willing to help others

Puts forth effort into all assignments

Working below grade level

Gets along well with peers

Very creative

Needs assistance with homework

Quality of work is improving

Displays a positive attitude

Enjoys socializing with classmates

Working above grade level

Follows classroom rules and directions

Working toward grade level

Disrupts class activities

Strong academic skills in the area of...

Demonstrates leadership qualities

Works well with others

Exceeds expectations

Needs extra practice with...

Always considerate of others

Participates in class activities

Self-confidence is improving

Has strong citizenship qualities

Has difficulty staying on task

A good listener

Enjoys taking risks

Conscientious worker

Likes to be challenged

Participates in class discussions

Demonstrating much growth in the area of…

> Every second we live is a new and unique moment of the universe, a moment that never was before and never will be again. And what do we teach our children in school? We teach them that 2 and 2 makes 4 and that Paris is the capital of France. When will we also teach them what they are? We should say to each of them: Do you know what you are? You are a marvel. You are unique. In all the world there is no other child exactly like you. In the millions of years that have passed there has never been a child like you. And look at your body what a wonder it is! Your legs, your arms, your cunning fingers, the way you move! You may become a Shakespeare, a Michelangelo, a Beethoven. You have the capacity for anything. Yes, you are a marvel. And when you grow up can you then harm another who is, like you, a marvel? You must cherish one another. You must work—we must all work—to make this world worthy of its children.
>
> **—Pablo Casals**

CLOSING WORDS

My first day as a first-grade teacher was full of the typical jitters. As the end of the day drew near, I had made it through most of the routines—reviewing rules, learning names, and so on. We were all exhausted. Then, quite unexpectedly and out of context, one of my students raised her hand. I called on her with curiosity, and I will never forget her simple three-word response. She said, "I love you," then went immediately back to her work. Those of us who commit our lives to the education of children recognize that intrinsic rewards are the best. We didn't choose to be teachers in order to get rich!

I think first grade is especially rewarding for many reasons. This is the year in which students learn to read and write. You witness it all coming together for a young boy or girl, and it just "clicks." They're reading for the first time! How exciting is *that?*

You build upon the skills learned in kindergarten and teach students to accomplish rather amazing tasks. Observing these victories on a daily basis reminds us how essential our jobs are.

Most importantly, we never forget how valuable these young individuals are. On average, I believe the progress students make during the first grade is unparalleled through their education. At the end of the year, after drying the tears from saying good-bye, you will walk away feeling a profound sense of accomplishment.

89

STAFF DIRECTORY AND CONTACT LIST

Position	Name	Office/Room No.	Contact
Principal			
Assistant Principal			
Secretary			
Office Assistant			
Custodian			
Cafeteria Worker			
Counselor			
Librarian			
Music Teacher			
Nurse			
Speech Teacher			
Psychologist			
P.E. Teacher			
Resource Teacher			
Student Assistants			
Kindergarten Teachers			
First-Grade Teachers			
Second-Grade Teachers			
Third-Grade Teachers			
Fourth-Grade Teachers			
Fifth-Grade Teachers			
Sixth-Grade Teachers			
Others			

VOLUNTEER SIGN-UP SHEET

Child's Name	Parent's or Guardian's Name	Phone Number	Address	How I Can Help (students, parties, preparation, field trips, etc.)

INFORMATION FOR MY SUBSTITUTE

My Name _____

Classroom Management

Classroom Rules:

"Quiet" Signal:

Possible Rewards:

Consequences:

Severe Consequences:

Get Help From:

Teacher: _____ Room #: _____

Teacher: _____ Room #: _____

Reliable Students:

Procedures

Beginning of the Day:

◆ Attendance:

◆ Lunch Money:

◆ Other:

Bathroom:

Drinking Fountain:

Hall:

Lunch:

Recess:

Dismissal:

Attached to This Sheet:

☐ Class List ☐ End of Day Report
☐ Seating Chart ☐ Daily Schedule
☐ Map of School ☐ Asst./Volunteer Info
☐ Bus List ☐ 5-Minute Ideas
☐ Adult Lunch Procedures
☐ Lesson Plans
☐ Reading and Math Groups
☐ Emergency Information
☐ School Rules ☐ Other:

Additional Comments/Information:

STUDENT INFORMATION SHEET

Name _____

Date _____

Birthday _____

Address _____

_____

_____

Phone number _____

(Photo or Drawing of Student)

Write or draw about your family.

Write or draw about things you like to do.

Write or draw things you want to do in the first grade.

Teacher: Have students complete this form twice: Once at the beginning of the year and once at the end. Include the beginning of the year information sheets in the portfolios of the individual students.

AWARD CERTIFICATE

Certificate of Achievement

This award is presented to:

_____

for successfully completing a
Reader's Workshop Project.

Congratulations!

_____

Teacher and Date